? ? ?

W T F

Victoria Lynn Morley's primary college degree is in psychology. Morley's intention with her trilogy of books is to get into the psyche of her own blood relatives and point out the irony of how they were killing each other based on religion, sex, ethnicity, jealousy, money or orders, such as war. Furthermore, she spread the trilogy from the early 1800s to present day, thereby illustrating how history is repeating itself. The same use of excessive force over and over. She essentially is trying to achieve coexistence and tolerance of each other's values. Achieving this without wars.

I dedicate this novel to my deceased family members.

Victoria Lynn Morley

Jack the Ripper

My Great Grandfather
Royal Assassin

Austin Macauley Publishers™
London • Cambridge • New York • Sharjah

A CIP catalogue record for this title is available from the British Library.

ISBN 9781528984980 (Paperback)
ISBN 9781528984997 (ePub e-book)

www.austinmacauley.com

First Published 2023
Austin Macauley Publishers Ltd®
1 Canada Square
Canary Wharf
London
E14 5AA

Preface

I was twelve years old in Mr Howard Stiles' science class at Lealman Middle School in St Petersburg, Florida. The assignment: to interview as many living family members as possible and come up with and write a paper on the most unusual, interesting, bizarre, amazing or horrifying family member. I was all hands-on deck. My grandma, Viola Raab told tales of a distant cousin sinking the Titanic. My great Aunt Bessie Benson told tales of her late husband, Howard being a detective in NYC busting Al Capone. My mother, Patricia Ellis told tales of her brother-in-law, Rolf Reinstorff being a Nazi and bombing London before he married her native-born English sister. My aunt, Ruth Holzhauser told tales of my Jewish great-great-grandfather from Germany coming to Ellis Island and becoming a diamond jeweller in NYC before the World Wars. In as much as I appeared intrigued, the stories kept coming.

I picked the "Titanic", it was appropriate for the seventh-grade class and they loved it. My great Aunt Bessie, however, was the best storyteller. I lived at 4680 and 47th St N St Petersburg, FL and she lived at 40th street and 3rd Ave N St Petersburg, FL, a modest bike ride away. I found myself frequently riding to her house and having tea in the yard while pondering over old photo albums. Her stories of our rich Malthouse Quaker family relatives from Brighton that owned a fleet of ships left me with more questions than answers as to what happened to the fortune.

At one point in time, when I was twenty-three, I had the opportunity to visit the Tabernacle in Salt Lake City, Utah. I already knew a bit of the Mormon religion and why they maintained and gathered a vast collection of archives of ancestry. My great Uncle Harold and Aunt Nellie were Mormons and taught me of the religious importance to research family. I took advantage of the opportunity to do research as in that era, 1987, it was before the internet. It was too difficult other than interviewing family to find the TRUTH. I learned quite a bit from that trip. Then, as members of the family would die, oddly I wound up inheriting special mementos or secret artefacts.

It wasn't until 2006 that I spread out all the pieces from England: Frederick Foster, the police architect of Scotland Yard's antique architectural kit. The Prince of Wales' Plumes Feather Pin with engraved initials of John Richard Malthouse; writing on the back of his photo, "Best swordsman, best shot, Afghan medal and fastest ¼ mile runner in the entire Calvary". Miniature bibles and small iconic inlaid wood star pieces, hand-carved Masonic looking gadgets and with many more family tales of holding a member of Scotland Yard hostage until his death. I put the clues together in sequence. I went on Ancestry.com, hired a private detective from London and with **motive, person, place, training, opportunity** and copies of Wills combined with family stories and a bit of imagination to make the book fiction, not boring faction. I began creating my first novel of a trilogy, using my own family members as the players.

I truly believe my great grandfather, John Richard Malthouse, was in fact "Jack the Ripper". It has been challenging and rewarding tracing his footprints back in time, from an offspring of an extremely religious pacifist sect of the Quakers in Brighton to evolving into the most fierce-some warrior in all of England's Royal Army, when London thought of itself as the "Capital of the World". I hope you as the reader will take a step back in time to the Victorian era and relive the past as I have, through the eyes of my blood relatives.

From the Author, Victoria Lynn Morley

Chapter 1

Quakers in Brighton (1802)

"Quiet, quiet please!" A man was shouting while standing in the front of a crowd of about fifty people and raising both arms up towards the ceiling of a small gathering room. "Friends, welcome. I've called this special meeting to order for a most important reason. It seems as though our Prince George *IV* wants to extend the garden of the Pavilion. I s'ppose the view out of the House just isn't acceptable to his royal likings. He's contacted the Malthouses and told them he's going to pay a fair amount for their land and knock down this building. The burial ground here will be paved over to make way for the 'New Road'. I'm not going to hold grudges against the Malthouses. I'm sure 'No' is not an acceptable answer to his Highness. Besides, we've outgrown this meeting house anyway. We give many thanks to our friends, the Malthouses for letting us meet here since back in 1716."

The crowd turned toward a small group of the Malthouse family and quietly applauded as the Malthouse family smiled and nodded their heads.

The speaker continued, "Over the last eighty-six years we've more than tripled in size. We can't fit all of the children in anymore. I thought it's about time enough to move our

Friends meeting to a more suitable place for the size of our group. The problem is, we don't have the luxury of leisure or time on our side now to make a lengthy decision because Prince George IV wants to begin immediately."

An old lady from the crowd shouted out in heckle, "The Prince hates Quakers; he just wants us off their land."

The man in the front quickly responded, "I don't believe that for a minute! Maybe they used to hate us, but they should be thankful now! Why, thanks to John Grover, we established one of the best boys' schools here! Why the Prince would have to be blind not to see that! We are a blessing to the community – we own most of the retail!"

"That's just it," another man yelled, "They hate us because they're jealous of us."

"Please stop all this nattering," the speaker said emphatically. "None of this helps the situation. Now, does anybody have any good ideas?"

A large man with a mop of unkempt red hair and a beard, wearing clothes that were scruffy and stained started pushing to the front. Addressing the group in a strong Irish brogue, he spouted out:

"I've been with you Friends now for a few years. I know I'm not much business-minded like some of you. I know you're probably thinking, 'He's only a butcher, what can he do?' But I own a piece of land, the ruins of St Bartholomew's Monastery. I bought the land for cheap because the locals think the land is sacred or haunted or something, or maybe they just don't want a Catholic church. But seeing how I was fresh off the boat from Ireland and still thought of myself as a Catholic, that was no problem for me. (O'course, that was b'for I joined you, Friends.)"

He paused for a breath and then continued: "The fig tree orchard still remains, but that's about it. The stones have all been plundered. The land would make a fine place for a new meeting hall and burial grounds. I'll offer this land for a fair price!"

He looked around for approval, and another member shouted with enthusiasm, "I know that land – it's perfect and I'm a stonemason. Why, with the help of a few others, I could build a new meeting hall!"

Other volunteers came forward from the group, and the decision was made to move quickly. The man presiding over the meeting again held up his arms, turned and said:

"Thank you Mr Glaisyer; it looks as though we will take you up on your offer, and with the help of the Lord, we'll have a fine new meeting hall."

Volunteers built the new hall in 1804. The windows were put up high on the wall to prevent distraction from prayers, and the benches went on either side of the aisle with a coke stove in the centre for warmth on cold days. They made a partition to separate the children from the central meeting. A hand-carved podium stood up front, positioned so that a speaker would face the group.

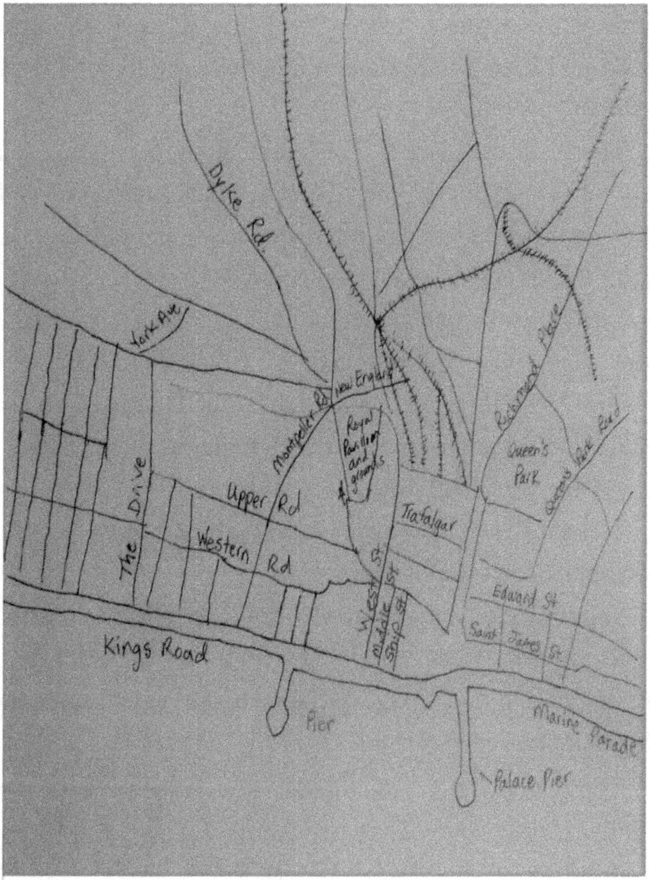

Brighton 1820s

More than two decades had passed since its completion, and by now the meeting hall was alive with people. The bride was getting ready in the partitioned area, and one older lady was saying, "He'll know what to do. They teach them that in their school, you know."

The nervous bride turned around when she heard this. Hardly anyone was sitting on 'her' side of the room for her family and friends according to tradition, however, 'his' side had many people.

The minister began the ceremony: "Do you John Malthouse take Mary Ann Sheehy…" and concluded with, "then on this fifteenth day of November, in the year 1825, of our Lord, I pronounce you man and wife."

The happy couple smiled at the congregation when they were leaving the meeting hall to embark on a new life together. Once they were alone, John turned to Mary and with pride told her that his parents were giving them the cottage.

"What cottage?" Mary asked in surprise.

Pleased that Mary looked happy about having her very own home, John went on to explain.

"The one outside the Royal Pavilion on the southeast corner of New Road. The Prince only knocked down the meeting hall to make way for the road, but he left the house. That's the bargain my parents made with him."

"You're codding me," Mary said, in a distinctly Irish brogue.

Smiling, John reached to touch her hand, "No, I'm serious. I'm taking you there right now."

And so, it was that John and Mary Malthouse started a life together in the 'Malt House Cottage' located on the grounds of the Royal Pavilion.

As John brought Mary up New Road to the Royal Pavilion, Mary gasped and exclaimed, "It's a castle!"

The Royal Pavilion

"Yes," replied John, "George IV had it built, it took seven years. They finished it three years ago. The famous John Nash was the architect, you know. Do you like the outside?"

Then, appearing to enjoy having special knowledge about the architect, John continued, "Supposedly, he tried to make it look Indian, and I hear the inside is Chinese."

"That sounds fascinating," Mary replied in a convincing tone.

John proceeded to explain how his Quaker parents had felt about the construction of the Pavilion.

"My parents couldn't stand all the construction – workmen trampling across our garden and all that, but mostly they complained about how many people needed money for food. With the money paid out to make it, they could have fed a lot of English people, and this wasn't the first time it happened. Originally, it was a farmhouse that the Prince leased from I don't know who. He spent twenty-two thousand pounds only to make it look French and then (soon after my parents sold him this land) he knocked down the old meeting hall along with half the farmhouse and then built this monstrosity."

"Well, I think it's just beautiful," Mary said, with eyes wide open and twinkling at the thought that this was to be the view from the window in her own home.

John tried to instil in his new wife the ways of the Quakers.

"Mary, the Lord does not want us to be overindulgent." He went on, "We should not take pride in material things; there are mouths to feed – this cannot provide for food. Our royalty robs the people of their hard, earned money!"

He turned away from the palace and walked toward a modest little cottage on the southeast side of the garden. "Now this is more like it," he chuckled, sweeping her up and carrying her across the threshold.

All night Mary dreamed of being a princess to distract herself from the pain she endured physically, as she willingly gave herself three times to her new husband, all the while staring out the window under the glow of a full moon. Through her romantic eyes, the palace gleamed enchantingly – so close across her garden.

John's family owned a fleet of merchant ships which was mainly for imports. John would go to sea for long periods at a time, and when he was leaving, Mary would walk with him down the New Road to Ship Street, then on to the docks where she would sadly wave to him as his vessel set sail for distant lands. Alone in the cottage, Mary felt forlorn that she had no child to care for and love.

Almost four years had passed before Mary bore the glow of a woman who has conceived a child. So very happy when she gave birth to a healthy baby girl, Mary could not wait for her husband's ship to return to port, and immediately had baby Emily christened at Saint Nicholas Church in Brighton on September 27, 1829. When John returned, and Mary told him of this, he was furious. (Mary had been born and raised in Ireland as a Catholic and had only converted to the Quaker Order to marry John. She wasn't wholly convinced about the ways of the Quakers, nor was she quite sure what their Catholic ways were.) Reproached by John, Mary hung her head and softly pleaded, "John, please don't be mad at me. I didn't know; I didn't know I did something wrong."

So, John decided that Mary needed counselling on the ways of the Quakers Society. He took Mary to his parents' cottage on Ship Street and asked his Mother to teach Mary the ways of the Quakers. As John's Mother would teach Mary, she would write down notes to remember all the rules. In her writings, she had a list of 16 things that could get a member cast out or disciplined by the church. She wrote as follows:

1. No one can be married by a hireling priest or minister either to another Quaker or someone not of the Society of Friends.
2. Fornication, having an illegitimate child or having a child too soon after marriage.
3. Marrying a cousin, or the sister or another relative of a wife who had died.
4. Drinking liquor to excess
5. Dancing
6. Gossiping
7. Attending another church, including the attendance of a wedding in another church.
8. Participating in the militia, supporting the military such as providing a horse, wagon, etc.
9. Paying taxes which supported the war or the Anglican Church.
10. Wearing fancy clothes
11. Engaging in activities which give way to vanity.
12. Swearing oaths as to your word in court or to government.
13. Taking off your hat to others.
14. Bad language
15. Failure to pay your debts.
16. Other

Mary was confused with all this teaching, especially since she could barely read or write and therefore needed assistance from her mother-in-law to be able to write this small list. After managing to write only fifteen prohibitions, Mary wrote "Other" – there were just too many things to write and remember.

Time slipped by as Mary spent her days playing with her beloved daughter, Emily, in the garden of their cosy cottage beside the Royal Pavilion. They dressed up with blankets as robes and made crowns out of vines, they would make up stories in which Emily was a princess and the Royal Pavilion was her palace. Mary had a child-like mind and appeared to be just as happy as Emily playing out these fantasy games.

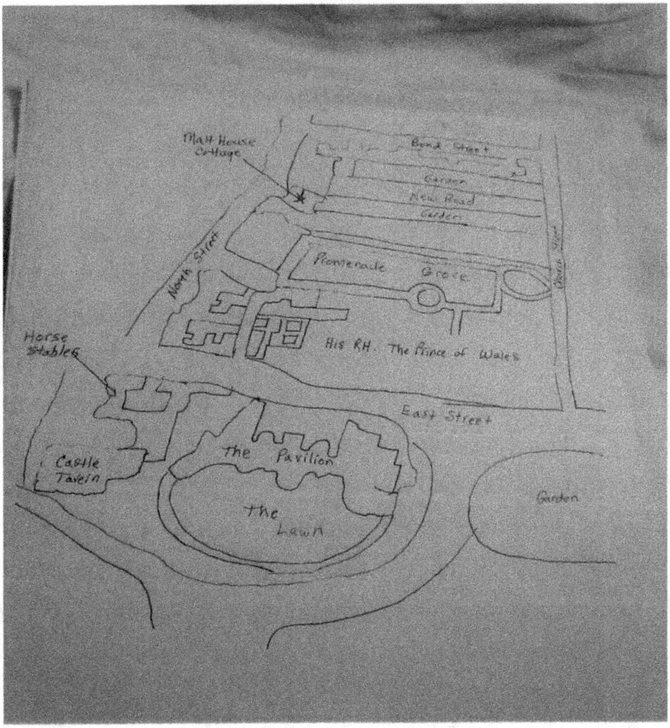

The Pavilion Grounds

Weeks turned into months and months into years until one day, when Emily had reached eleven years of age, the two were playing their favourite game of 'queens and kings' when an elegant procession approached on the New Road. Emily and Mary just stood to stare in wonder as a splendid carriage, drawn by six regal horses, stopped in front of the Palace and an aristocratic young man appeared at the carriage door. He held himself very erect and proud as he carefully stepped out of the carriage. Emily and Mary ran their eyes over his dark brown hair, beguiling (yet intense) eyes, short brown moustache, cleft chin and the tight pants that emphasized his firm, well-developed buttocks and thighs. Mary turned to Emily and, with heart pounding in her chest and sounding as if she were about to swoon, she blurted out, "He's absolutely gorgeous."

Then, raising her voice, exclaimed, "Who is he?"

The nobleman, hearing a female voice, turned and looked in their direction. When he saw the two draped in blankets that appeared to mimic royal robes, he could not contain a laugh. Then, in a playful gesture of joining in their game, he waved at them in a circular motion while dramatically bowing forward, as a Spanish cavalier might do. Just then, a pale, feminine hand reached out from the carriage; kissing it, he helped a lady step out. The elegant lady with the pale hand glowered in the direction of those who had been honoured by the nobleman's playfulness, prompting Mary to clasp her face with both hands and exclaim, "Oh my, that's the Queen! Come on now, Emily; we'd better get inside."

The two then quickly ran into their cottage and peered out the window.

"That's Queen Victoria," Mary explained to Emily, "the one we've seen here a couple of times before. And that must be her new prince, Prince Albert. Everybody's been talking about him. The people around here aren't happy because he's a German. But he's breath-taking, so it's no wonder she married him."

Emily's mom then fell back on the bed exclaiming, "Oh, that I were Queen Victoria and that he (Albert) was my prince."

Sighing, she then stared at the ceiling with the dreamiest pools for eyes that Emily had ever seen. Somewhat mystified by her mother's actions, Emily impishly tickled mommy's tummy for a moment, and then the two of them danced in the middle of the floor. It was at that very moment that John opened the door and with horror exclaimed, "Mary, what are you doing, dancing is frowned upon by the Lord, and take those blankets off, they look ridiculous."

"We've just seen the new prince and Queen Victoria," wide-eyed, uncontrollably-smiling, Mary blurted out.

"Wipe that smile off your face. I am not impressed by the Queen," John retorted.

"It's not the Queen I was talking about," smirked Mary while Emily giggled in the background. John pretended not to notice, but an air of tension squelched any further talk, and at dinner, they ate in virtual silence. Mary and Emily grew accustomed to seeing the Prince and Queen at the Pavilion during various times of the year. They would frequently see the Prince standing on the veranda gazing over in their direction, and they somehow felt that he was watching over them.

When Emily turned thirteen, she got her mother's permission to help out at the palace as a servant. The palace was always in need of help. Her father would not be made aware of this, and whenever John came home earlier than expected, Mary would provide an adequate alibi for Emily when she wasn't home. After her first chance to tour the palace, Emily couldn't wait to rush home and tell her mother all about it. She had entered the palace through an archway that led into a large octagonal room. Full-length windows in the room permitted the light to flood in, even lighting up the entrance hall and the adjoining rooms. The ceiling gave her the impression of being in a tent with bowed down and drawn up plaster, as with tent tie poles. The walls had blue and white paintings of Asian scenes, and a large marble fireplace attracted Emily's attention. From the octagon room, she went down a long corridor (probably around one hundred fifty feet long) which had skylights overhead for light during the day and candle lanterns or oil lamps for lighting at night. This corridor led to the banquet room, the music room, the drawing-room and Prince Albert's bedroom. Robert Jones decorated the banquet room. It was breath-taking with its domed ceiling (painted like a tree) reaching about forty-five feet into the sky. Hanging down about fifteen feet from this domed ceiling was an enormous chandelier with copper leaves and a menacing silver dragon with claws clutching the crystals that decorated the light. In the corners of the room, there were smaller gasoliers for lighting with lotus leaf bowls and then all around the room, there were large porcelain columns with engravings of ormolu and giltwood rising to form a lotus blossom. Rosewood sideboards dotted the room with gilded dragons holding candles and serving bowls. Beside the banquet room was the decker's room where Emily worked. This room was a sort of a 'go-between' for the banquet room and the great kitchen. Emily would serve the food brought in from the kitchen by the chefs, and later she would clear the tables from this area until there was enough room in the kitchen to fit all the dirty dishes. The kitchen was huge, supported by cast iron and copper palm tree columns. As one would expect, the working spaces and the appliances here were all state-of-the-art. Off the corridor was the south drawing-room with its pink and gold decorated walls and its gold giltwood dolphin furniture.

The north drawing-room had trompe l'oeil paintings of gold leaves on the walls and columns wrapped with gilded dragons. The furniture in this room was of Rococo style.

Then, finally, there was the music room which had been decorated by Frederick Crace. The room was as big as the banquet room but even more impressive, as it had lotus-shaped gasoliers which lit up the walls where red crimson and gold landscape scenes were meticulously painted. It, too, had a domed ceiling which was surrounded by scalloped shells. An ornate porcelain pagoda and a dragon chimneypiece of white marble stood out in the room, surrounded by oriental dark rosewood furniture. Over and over again, Emily's mother would make Emily describe the palace as she first saw it. Emily seemed to realise that her mother did this because she was basically illiterate and therefore unable to enjoy the pleasure of reading. Having Emily describe the elegance of the Pavilion allowed her to visualise and memorise each detail so that she could mentally write her books about her pretend life with the Prince in the palace.

One day, as Emily was working in the kitchen, Prince Albert surprised her.

"Emily, that is your name, is it not?" Emily shook with awe.

"Yes, yes, Your Majesty, that's my name."

"I want you to meet somebody, follow me," the Prince ordered as he turned and walked upstairs. Emily had never been upstairs before and therefore had never seen any of the bedrooms.

Where is he taking me and why? she fearfully wondered.

Though uncertain of his intentions, she dutifully followed him up the stairs and into one of the bedrooms. Imagine her relief when she saw a sleeping baby in a bassinet. The Prince put his finger over his mouth and pursed his lips in a motion to be quiet, followed by a whispered, "This is my son, Albert Edward VII – isn't he beautiful?"

Albert spoke with the pride of a new father. Emily could feel her face turning red with embarrassment about initial doubts of his intentions. Prince Albert pretended not to notice, though she suspected that he had read her mind. "The Queen doesn't care much for babies and is in need of some quiet time," the Prince continued. "She stays in her room down the hall much of the time. The nursemaids are available when they are needed. However, they're not well educated. I hear that your reading and writing is perfect and that you have studied the sciences and sociology also, is that correct?"

"Yes, Your Highness," stuttered Emily.

"Good," said Prince Albert, "English is my second language, and I wish my son to grow up with impeccable English grammar. He's going to be the king one day, you know. So beginning immediately, when I am here at the Pavilion, I wish for you to be his nanny. I want you to be his tutor."

"But he's only a baby," Emily incredulously replied.

"That doesn't matter," said the Prince, "I will write you a set of instructions each time, beginning with this very weekend."

With that, Albert took out a piece of paper and wrote on it:

1. *Sing nursery rhymes to him while he is awake.*
2. *Dancing with Albert is permitted in the music room only.*

Emily looked shocked when she read this and stammered, "But I can't dance with you!"

"Shhhhh, not me, the baby," Albert quietly laughed. "I'll just call him Bertie so you won't get confused."

The Prince appeared somehow pleased as well as amused by the thought that this thirteen-year-old girl had imagined that he wanted to dance with her. Then he instructed, "I'd like for you to stay in the bedroom next to the Prince's room, I mean Bertie's room when you are here."

Emily and her mother had a sweet, close relationship and her mother wanted to hear all about everything that happened at the palace. Mary was proud and thrilled that whenever the royal family was visiting Brighton, her daughter would be a nanny to the boy who would one day be the next king of England. She assured Emily that she would break the news to her father very gently. When she broached the subject that evening, upon hearing that Emily was going to work for the royal family, John first protested, but then relented as he thought how this could be proper training for his daughter.

As the years passed, Prince Albert introduced Emily to three more newborns. By the time Emily was sixteen, she was guiding four children, although Bertie was always her primary pupil. Sad to say that although Victoria was Queen of England, she nevertheless was miserable during her many pregnancies. Feeling fat and ugly, she would slip into a depression much of the time. Feelings of jealousy also gripped her that Albert would choose to spend so much of his time with the children (rather than spending time with her) and she was aware of his fascination with the young nanny. She pleaded with Albert not to have the children accompany them on any of their vacations away from London.

Unmoved, Albert insisted on bringing the children to the shore at Brighton, explaining that Emily was a nanny for the very purpose of caring for the children. Searching for other excuses, Victoria then complained about lack of privacy in Brighton due to the trains, which could now bring people quickly from London for only one pound. She suggested putting a wall around the gardens so that the people who lived in the houses could not peer into their property and perhaps it would be even better to knock the houses down.

The Queen recalled how the former King George IV had enjoyed a secret affair with a lady who lived in one of the houses across the garden, where Emily was living, so conveniently close to Albert. Never wanting to express her fears to Albert, Victoria suggested going to the Isle of Wight (a small island in the English Channel) instead of spending time in Brighton.

"It will afford us more privacy," she urged.

And so, it was, the once grand Pavilion began to fall into disrepair. Undeterred by his wife's wishes, Prince Albert had Emily transported to the Isle of Wight by one of her father's ships so that she could continue to join the family vacations as a nanny to the children.

Chapter 2

Prince Albert Seduces Emily

One evening, when Albert and Victoria arrived at the dock in preparation for a trip to the Isle of Wight, the Prince became alarmed when he couldn't find Emily. Concerned, he quickly asked the dock staff (including Emily's cousin):

"Where's Emily?"

"She's at the Malt House Cottage," replied one of the boys. "She's eighteen now, and I think her father's trying to make arrangements for her to go to college. She won't be working for Your Highness anymore."

Prince Albert turned to Victoria and with urgency in his voice said, "Go on without me, and I'll see if I can fetch her."

The Prince then took a horse and rode up to the little Malt House Cottage, where Mary answered the door.

"Oh, Your Highness," she stammered (while bowing to his majesty), "If it's Emily you're wanting, she is in the bathtub."

The Prince without a word of explanation commanded, "Tell her when she gets out to come over to the palace. I need to talk to her, I've been blessed with yet another child."

"Oh, that makes five now then," Mary exclaimed in excitement.

The Prince remounted his horse and continued up to the Pavilion to wait for Emily, where the stable was attached to the palace. As soon as the Prince left, Mary hurried to Emily and started pulling her out of the bath.

"Hurry up, you can't keep him waiting," Mary told Emily, as she helped her pull on her dress. Emily raced out the door and across the garden. As she ran toward the front entrance, out of the corner of her eye, she noticed the Prince standing at the entrance to the stable. She stopped running immediately, turned and walked over toward the stable. As she approached the Prince, she began to apologise for not having been at the dock, but Prince Albert thought on more intimate things as he gazed on the Emily he now saw before him.

He had watched her grow, and now she was entirely a woman. Her long red hair was still wet and clung to her damp, now see-through white dress. Drops of water were glistening on her fair white bosom. Having run so far, she was panting heavily. With her youthful, perfect complexion and gleaming blue eyes, Albert found himself captivated. Without thinking, he reached out and gently touched her cheek.

"I hear you are going to leave us," he said in a soft, sad voice.

Emily was excited by Albert's touch and gazing into his dark brown eyes she whispered, "Yes, my father is sending me to Chichester to the girls' college there. It's a Quaker college where he thinks I'll get the best education."

"That's too bad," Albert murmured, as he edged closer to her while still touching her cheek. "I'm going to miss you, my Emily."

He leaned forward and gently kissed her lips. Blushing to the point that even her bosom was blotched and mottled,

Emily pulled back and stood up. Albert couldn't take his eyes from her now pulsating breast. Trying to pull herself together, Emily cleared her throat, smiled and asked about the new baby.

"Yes," replied Albert, "I have another daughter that we have named Louise, but I didn't come here to talk about Louise, I came here to talk to you."

He made a motion to be quiet and then began kissing her lips and holding the back of her head with his left hand. He started to kiss her mouth deeply, inserting his tongue as his right hand began to caress her left cheek. Trembling, Emily found herself kissing him back even more intensely. Slowly and carefully he began to unbutton the front of her dress with his right hand, carefully pulling the top open to expose her beautiful white breasts and erect pink nipples. Stooping, he gently kissed her willing lips and then, licking his lips, he gazed at her lovely bosom.

"Have you ever seen my bedroom, Emily?" he whispered.

"No," Emily whispered back, as if in a trance.

"Would you like to see my bedroom now, Emily?"

Again, as if under his spell, Emily whispered, "Yes."

Emily and the Prince walked hand in hand into the palace. Once inside, the Prince lit a candle and (almost as if in a dream) they continued up the stairs and down the great corridor to his bedroom. Slowly, he opened the door to a dark room where the furnishings were hard to distinguish. It appeared to Emily as though they were walking through some library before entering the boudoir of the Prince. Though hard to determine, the walls seemed to be a shade of blue on which dragons, birds, flowers and things of that nature had been painted. But the bed was the only thing on which Emily could focus. It was a massive four-poster bed with carvings in dark wood. Old curtains hung from a canopy, and the Prince slowly opened these curtains to expose blue satin linens covering the bed.

Letting go of Emily's hand, the Prince circled the room lighting candles. As he did so, Emily could hear her breathing getting faster and harder until she feared she couldn't get enough air and might even faint. The Prince returned to the foot of the bed where he began to slowly take off Emily's dress as he also removed his attire. Emily could feel herself begin to burn as he gently pressed his muscular chest against hers, again holding the back of her head with his left hand and gently pressing his lips to hers. For the first time, this young woman experienced an excitement never before known to her as the burning became an almost 'aching' between her legs. The muscles there began to contract and release, and she felt warm moisture trickling down her thigh. She felt in a euphoric trance. The Prince had been caressing her breast, but now he moved his hand down to her thigh (just beneath the spot where she felt the aching') and knew that he, too, must be aware of her wet female response to his caresses. He left his right hand on her upper thigh for so long that Emily couldn't stand it anymore and placing her hand over his, she moved his hand to that spot of euphoric joy. Slowly, (no, too slowly) he gently rubbed the spot in a circular motion and carefully leaned her over backwards onto the bed. With the Prince towering over her, Emily inched her way up to the top of the bed, responding passionately to the lips now pressed so hard against her own as he continued to caress that special spot between her legs. This ardent Prince now pulled her right leg over him, causing them both to roll over on their sides, the Prince whispered in a passionate voice, "Are you sure you want to do this, Emily?"

Entranced entirely, Emily could only whisper, "Yes."

Only then did the Prince slowly insert himself into her. It was all so dreamlike, as he moved her into various positions with graceful, ballet-like motions and spellbound, she had no concern for her inexperience. Then finally he laid forcefully on top of her and with his pelvis thrusting faster and faster, he went deeper inside her than before. She could feel the muscles of her vagina clamping down on him and realised she was holding her breath – she couldn't breathe, but she couldn't keep from breathing either. Emily knew that if she didn't hold her breath that the aching would only increase, get worse and worse (or better and better). Finally, the most fantastic sensation came over her, like a sneeze that had been pent up for a lifetime. When this happened, she moaned with both pleasure and pain. Instantly, the Prince did the same, as if almost an echo. Then they rested as spent lovers.

Emily was having sex for the first time with the only man she would ever love. The Prince lay on top of her, inside her while they caught their breaths. When their breathing had slowed, Emily suddenly became fearful.

The Prince sensed Emily's fear and reassured her with the words, "I love you, Emily. I have loved you from the day I first saw you in that silly blanket, pretending to be my Princess. Then I watched you grow into the most beautiful woman. I watched you from the balconies. I watched you playing with Bertie while I wished it was me. But I am married to the Queen; I am a slave to her. There's too much pressure from every direction for me to ever divorce her. You understand I must remain married to the Queen."

Emily began to cry and sorrowfully asked, "What do we do now?"

The Prince reassured her saying: "You go back to your mother and do not mention anything. I'll tell Victoria that you went off for college. Tell your parents you want one more year here at home before going to college, but will not be staying on as our nanny. Victoria will know. We'll look for a new tutor for Bertie – I've been thinking about recruiting a young man from Cambridge named Henry Birch. Bertie's been slipping further behind Arthur and Alice in his studies, and maybe this man can straighten him out. Maybe this will turn out for the better. When I'm in town, I'll send for you, and we'll meet here, in the palace since it is empty now. I'll tell Victoria I'm gathering up artworks or something – she'll never suspect anything."

After they both had dressed, the Prince went about the room blowing out the candles. Then they walked hand in hand back up the corridor, kissing farewell before opening the entrance door, each then going a separate way.

Emily went home, but unlike before when she and her mother shared everything, she could not discuss this with her now. Emily had to implore her father to be allowed to remain at home for one more year before starting college;

"The Prince needs me for this last baby," she explained.

Although illiterate, Emily's mother was not blind to the behaviour of a daughter who was infatuated with a man. Her mother loved her deeply. However, she thought it wise to keep her beliefs to herself and even succeeded in talking Emily's father into allowing her one more year at home.

Emily's relationship with Albert became a torrid love affair. Emily secretly believed that the Prince would one day leave Victoria and then marry her, so the drive to make him love her fuelled the fire between them even more. Thus, each secret encounter became even more passionate than the one before.

Albert was aware of a secret backdoor in the Prince Regent's Boudoir and he and Emily delighted in a cat and mouse chase when they thought they were alone. But Victoria (unpersuaded by Albert's inadequate reasons) had become suspicious of his obsession with going alone to an empty palace in Brighton, so occasionally she would arrive without notice.

It wasn't long before Emily realised she was with child. Young, without guidance and mentoring, inexperienced, she was too blinded by love to be careful. She seemed lost between rules of behaviour: staunch Quaker and Catholic. If Emily could have only had a worldly advisor who truly cared for her happiness, she may have been guided through this moral maze which in the end deprived her of all she deserved in life.

Albert persuaded Emily not to tell her parents and instead to say that she was travelling with the royal family. Albert arranged for Emily to serve as a maid in a private house in London for nine long months following which she gave birth to a baby girl at the St George Hanover Square Infirmary. In deciding on a name for their little love-child, Albert thought Emily's middle name, Adelaide, would be a good choice. As to the authorities documenting the birth, Emily provided false information, stating that she, herself, had been born in London, giving birth to baby Adelaide, 'father unknown'. Now torn between her love for her child and the still-burning love she carried for Albert, Emily sadly placed little Adelaide in a London workhouse, where nuns would care for her. She then went home to her parents in Brighton where she and Albert could continue their love affair.

Albert would secretly check on the welfare of Adelaide by visiting the workhouse from time to time. These visits made him suddenly focus on the health of the poor and needy and served as an excellent excuse to keep visiting Adelaide.

Emily and Albert returned to the joys of their secret rendezvous in Brighton at the Royal Pavilion, where Emily particularly revelled in making love in the music room, which had been the favourite room of her majesty, the Queen. More and more, the Queen became aware of Albert's loss of caring for her. He acted preoccupied with other interests and unaffectionate to the point of treating her in a distant, almost cold manner. Soon her suspicions of infidelity overcame her and one day, while back at the palace in London, she casually remarked, "Albert, I've sold the Royal Pavilion in Brighton."

"Don't do it!" Albert shouted.

"It's too late; I already have," she proclaimed, with a hidden delight at his torment.

"My God, why did you do that," Albert burst out in distress.

Trying to appear indifferent in her response, the Queen casually responded, "I didn't care much for the architecture," and in a sweeping motion, she walked away.

In Victorian times, it was almost permissible to have affairs, just as long as they were discreet. Queen Victoria, however, was not only filled with jealousy, but it was common knowledge that she had a terrible temper. So, that was as close as they needed to come to talking about Albert's infidelity.

The Prince was determined and still held a strong desire for young Emily and a few days later, informed Victoria that he had plans to hold a world fair in England. He would build the most impressive palace of glass and have articles from all over the world shipped in for display there.

The next time he met with Emily in Brighton, after a short embrace she pulled back and in a voice of nervous agitation exclaimed, "They sold the Pavilion. I went over to see what all the commotion was about and the city people informed me that they are the new owners and it is to become a museum! They said I could work as a tour director and that they want to turn our house into a tea cottage. Oh, Albert, when will I ever see you?"

With that, she began to cry.

"Cheer up," Albert said, "I'll be coming here a lot. I'm going to have a fair, a world's fair. I'll be making arrangements to have merchandise shipped here from all over the world. Have no fear, my love; we will see a lot of each other."

"Oh, you can ask my father if you can hire his fleet of ships," Emily exclaimed excitedly. Now she was smiling and jumping up and down.

When Emily went home, she told her father all about the fair and how the Prince wished to hire the service of his ships. She told him that there would be displays of art and science, new machinery and so much more and that for the first time the world would be united in the quest to further industrial and scientific advancement. Emily couldn't contain herself at the thought and the knowledge that she would be able to continue to see her Prince.

Her father, on the other hand, cautioned, "Emily the Quakers have suffered at the hands of royalty for decades. Nothing good has ever come from helping them as they are simply users. They take what they can get, they suck you dry and then they throw you out to sea when you are no longer useful to them. I will not willingly engage in helping this Prince attain his goal to world fame for this fair. It is absolutely out of the question. The Lord would look down upon us."

Emily and Mary were very disappointed, and Emily began to cry. But her tears could not overcome her father's religious upbringing, and he sternly declared, "No. And that's final."

Weeks had passed since that sad day, and Emily was now conducting a tour of the Royal Pavilion when one of the nursemaids who had befriended Emily was sent by the Prince to lead her through the secret underground tunnel that connected the Royal Pavilion to a nearby hotel. The passion between the lovers was not over, and Emily joyfully hurried to the Prince's embrace.

When, as was their custom, they talked after quenching their lustful cravings, Emily told Albert, "My father won't allow you the use of our ships. He says it goes against God's will."

The Prince, inflamed by this, quickly replied, "I rather thought that such was the case when I did not hear from him. Well, you can tell your father that I have decided to make a new road (which will be called 'Prince Albert Street') and that it's going to go right through his house. So, it would be well if he started right now to look for a new home. Also, I have already begun making arrangements for docks on my own – 'The Great Grimsby docks'. I have donations for a few ships too, and in fact, that might just put your father right out of business. Stupid Quakers, we should ship the rest of them off to the Americas!"

Albert's temper was getting the better of him. This was the first time Emily had seen his rage and desire for retribution.

A long time passed before Albert returned to the Pavilion and the nursemaid came to fetch Emily. Albert was already waiting naked in the bed, and Emily came forward slowly, whispering in a sad voice, "Albert, look at my belly, I'm going to have a baby again."

Albert stood up, hastily dressed and announced:

"I can't handle this right now. I'm too busy building this magnificent palace of glass, and half the people don't seem to understand its importance. They are more concerned with keeping the grass in Hyde Park. It was supposed to open this month and this is too much for me to deal with. This time you are going to have to take care of it yourself."

In shocked disbelief, Emily burst into tears as she reached out for her Prince to reassure and hold her. Falling to the floor, she clung to his legs as he strode towards the doorway.

"Please, you can't leave me, I can't do this on my own," pleaded poor Emily.

Stopping for a moment, the Prince spewed out a litany of reasons why he could not participate in helping Emily in her present time of need.

"Half the city of London is ready to shoot me because they're worried I cater to atheists and religious zealots that are enraged because I was suggesting knighting Charles Darwin for his brilliant theory of evolution. They are also in anti-papal debates over the appointment of Cardinal Nicholas Wiseman.

The Prime Minister's horse just fell on him and killed him. Emily, I don't sleep at night, and you can't handle one simple pregnancy by yourself. Did you really believe we were going to last forever? Life is not a fantasy, and you are never going to be a princess!" Having said that, the Prince walked out of Emily's life for the last time.

Distraught, Emily wandered back to the secret passageway, fearful that she would never see her Prince and lover again. A couple of weeks later, the city delivered the official notification to one named John Malthouse, Esquire (Emily's father) that the cottage on the grounds of the Royal Pavilion was to be evacuated immediately, per orders of his majesty, Prince Albert so that it could be made into a café. John and Mary decided to move in with John's mother on Ship Street. However, it turned out that the Prince had notified the city officials of his plan to have a new street built that would go right through the area now occupied by the house of John's Mother. This new road was to be named 'Prince Albert Road'.

Consequently, they all moved in with one of John's brothers who also lived on Ship Street. After they moved in, and Emily, still not having heard from the Prince, knew she would have to tell her mother about the coming baby soon as she could not hide it much longer.

When the appropriate moment arrived, Emily tearfully confessed, "Mother, I have done something very, very, bad."

Mary immediately began to cry with Emily as she responded, "Don't tell me, Emily, I fear what you are about to say."

Emily, needing to complete her confession, continued, "Mother, I am carrying the Prince's baby."

"Oh, good Lord", cried Mary. "It's all my fault; it's all because I played those stupid games with you and made you think you could become a real princess one day. It's my fault. It's all my fault. Oh God, what shall we tell your father?"

When John returned from the sea, it was necessary to tell him immediately. Shocked and distraught with sorrow mixed with anger, John thundered:

"That Prince has caused us nothing but problems. He took our land, he's taking away my business and now he's ruined our daughter! God, Emily has damned us! You have damned the family into hell with your wickedness! I want you to leave this house immediately – I don't have a daughter anymore."

Both Mary and Emily fell to the floor at John's feet, weeping and begging him not to disown Emily. Hearing all the commotion, Emily's grandmother came up and convinced her son to take the issue to the Friends meeting house, saying, "We will let God decide what to do."

Later, a small, solemn group gathered at the meeting house. After addressing the gathering, the minister turned to Emily and, in a puritanical tone, admonished her.

"Emily, you have broken many of our most sacred laws. You have forsaken your family and brought ill upon the entire community. We are losing our jobs because of this Prince. Many of us are having to learn new trades, like building train engines, storing ice, opening public houses – things we never imagined we would have to do. The wrath of God is upon us! Your unborn child was not to blame. You are. You may stay until you have the child, but then you must leave Brighton for good and never return."

On December 3rd 1851, Emily gave birth to a baby boy, whom she named John Richard Malthouse, after her father.

When the baby was three months old and strong enough to survive, Emily and her baby boy had to leave her home and community. Her situation was against Quaker rules; she had to be banished.

Chapter 3

Emily's Exile from Brighton's Quakers

Not knowing where to go or how to support herself, she took a train to London and went directly to the palace, where she demanded to see the Prince. After being advised that Prince Albert was away attending to the Crystal Palace at the World's Fair, Emily began blurting out that this baby was his, but she was quickly ushered into a small room. An official at the palace then came in, and Emily explained that she had been a nanny to young Prince Bertie when the royal family spent time in Brighton. Bertie, now nine years old, was summoned but, as he ran towards her with arms outstretched to hug his former loving nanny, he was quickly restrained and removed from the room. Emily was then escorted from the palace grounds and taken to the St George Hanover Square workhouse (where she had previously abandoned baby Adelaide) because the officials believed that she had been born in London rather than Brighton. The officials then informed the workhouse staff that Emily was attempting to extort money from Prince Albert by claiming that he fathered her baby. They continued that she was an insane pauper prostitute from the east end slum of London. The staff all had a good laugh at her story. It was all too much for Emily, and she began to suffer a nervous breakdown. At times, she would demand that the staff contact the Prince and notify him of her whereabouts, but this resulted in more laughter and ridicule with returns of, "Yes, your majesty Princess Emily."

To cope with her surroundings, Emily resorted to a fantasy world, eventually not being sure what the truth was. The staff enjoyed the fun of mockingly calling her 'Princess', but this princess had to earn her keep by binding books and performing chores at the workhouse.

It was a harsh life for the unfortunate people of London who found themselves 'warehoused' in one of these overcrowded, under-ventilated workhouses. Densely populated, children were packed four or five (sometimes six) to a bed and were frequently afflicted with a fever.

Only two meals of meat a week were served. This was survival of the fittest in its full force, and many children were dying.

Prince Albert did visit the workhouse, from time to time. The palace was only a few blocks away. He would only view them from a distance so as not to bring any attention to the fact that he was there. He covered his visits with the excuse that he was looking into the possibility of improving the condition of the pauper houses. He could see Emily's brain had already succumbed to a degree of insanity; she didn't know the truth anymore, but his daughter, Adelaide was healthy and doing well. John was also an intelligent, ambitious child. He was attempting to learn his reading and writing skills to the best of his abilities. He was taught to say his catechisms by the nuns. The sisters frequently told John that he was the bastard son of a prostitute and would bear the burden of his mother's sinful life.

When John was ten, Prince Albert made his final visit. Upon Prince Albert's return to the palace, the royal doctor confirmed Prince Albert as having come down with fever or typhoid from that wretched workhouse. Prince Albert was becoming weaker by the hour and feared his death, he called for his son Bertie who was now a twenty-year-old man. Albert said, "Bertie, I fear for my death. I need to tell you a misdeed I have committed. Do you remember Emily, your nanny in Brighton?"

"Yes father, I do" replied Bertie.

"She bore two children of mine. A boy and a girl. John and Adelaide Malthouse. Please keep an eye on them for me. Enlist the boy in our cavalry when he is old enough. Forgive me son but don't breathe a word of this to your mother. Promise me."

"Yes father, I promise" replied Bertie, as he stood by the bedside of his dying Father. Albert died December 14th 1861, at Windsor Castle.

Chapter 4

The Fall out After Prince Albert's Death

When the staff at St George told Emily that Prince Albert had died, they thought it might snap her out of her delusions yet instead this drove her into further insanity as now she had no hope left in life. She wrote to her parents in one last desperate plea for help. Her father, John had already died. However, her mother, Mary was still alive. She was feeling terrible and responsible for what had become of her only daughter Emily, and the mother arranged to have a cousin move to London and live with Emily and try to take care of her. Although Mary had the urge to, it was against the Quaker religion to blackmail anyone. The Quaker community wouldn't allow Emily's return; So, Emily would continue to suffer, without financial assistance. All Mary could do was send Emily a cousin, James Malthouse. James was a good looking young man, only eighteen years of age. He had been born at sea and led a life of a sailor. He was tan and robust but lacked potential, intellectually, to carry on the family business. When James arrived at the workhouse, he found Emily almost dead as she had quit eating from the depths of her depression. James found some eight hundred or more people living in that wretched place. He requested an immediate transfer and they were moved to the St Pancras workhouse.

Bertie, however, had already checked into the condition of the family and had asked that John move into the country for fresh air. A Methodist minister widower took John under his custody.

John was a beautiful, smart ten-year-old little boy and frequently found himself forced into the object of the widower's sexual desire. This was unfortunately then compounded by the widower's shame, as he was a devout Methodist minister, so John was then physically abused because of this. The minister had transferred the blame of his wickedness onto John. This sexual and physical abuse went on for three long years before the wicked man died.

During Emily's time at St Pancras, although initially she was only taught to spine books, it evolved into making clothes. She had found an outlet for which she had talent. James was such a strong man that he worked as a porter at the local market. James talked the Malthouse family into sending him enough money to buy a small shop for Emily.

Construction of a new row of houses had just been completed with warehouses and docks nearby. It was the perfect place for Emily and him. They moved into #9 Buck's Row. Emily set up a Hosiers and named it 'Malt House Cottage'. She was the head dress-maker and Adelaide, then a young sixteen-year-old girl, became a seamstress. James worked across the street at the warehouses. John was only a fourteen-year-old boy. He would walk to Christchurch workhouse where he would continue his education and religious training. Emily was happy with the Christchurch as they offered Quaker training and had a Quaker cemetery. When John wasn't at the church, he would wander across the small alley into the stable yard with the horses. He was paid a few pennies to muck out the horse stalls there. As he hadn't had any affection or emotional closeness from anyone in his life before, he took to the horses. He was very good with the horses. He could communicate on a level with them that most others couldn't. But times were hard and money was even harder to come by. Next door to the stables was the horse slaughterers. As much as he hated to, he had to appeal to them for some work.

He learned how to slaughter the horses. And back at the stables, he was taught how to shoe the horses. He became so good at making the shoes and working with the smouldering metal that he made other sorts of metal objects. He had become an expert silversmith. He hated the slaughtering of the horses as it was too slow. The knives were too dull. So, he made his own knives for the slaughter. He would cut their throats quickly and skilfully so that they would not suffer. And then he would embrace them until their silent death. He always made sure that he severed their vocal cords, as their whinnying cries haunted his dreams. Then he would carve up their carcasses for the much-needed meat. He too needed their flesh for his food.

Such was John's teenage existence. He viewed his mother as a pathetic individual who bore him out of wedlock yet still maintained stories about him being the son of the former Prince. He knew this not to be true, as his sister, Adelaide, had been all but abandoned there at St George for more than two years. The staff used to warn him about his whore mother. He knew his mother didn't love either one of them, and she never expressed anything but remorse that either one of them should ever have been born. And James wasn't Emily's husband, as she tried to pass him off as. John released these emotions of hatred and contempt for his mother. While he carved up the horses, he would think about her work in her shop right there across the alley.

They slept at various lodging houses when they had enough money as the shop afforded little privacy and comfort for the family. They were lodging with a family on John Street when a knock resounded on the door. A young man was standing fully suited up in a soldier's uniform when Adelaide answered the door.

"I have papers for John Richard Malthouse," said the soldier.

"What on earth for?" Questioned Adelaide, as she gazed at the young man in uniform. He replied, "Prince Albert Edward wishes to enlist him in the military. He is to report for duty this Monday."

"He's over at the slaughter yard on Buck's Row," replied Adelaide.

"Well, see to it he gets this," said the soldier sternly and then he turned and left.

Adelaide knew she shouldn't tell her mother this, as Quaker's are pacifists and are opposed to any military support, much less joining one. So, Adelaide ran over to the slaughterhouse herself with the papers. Adelaide was a young, beautiful, twenty-year-old woman now and John was a strapping, handsome eighteen-year-old boy.

"John, John," Adelaide began calling as soon as she entered the stable yards. Her long Victorian dress was getting covered with mud as she ran through the puddles.

It was raining. When John answered, "Over here."

She turned and fell right in the muck of the horse stables. John had been communicating or whispering to the horse; he was standing beside it, stroking its neck.

"The Prince, the Prince wants you for the military. Maybe all of mother's crazy stories were right. Maybe Prince Albert was our Father. Oh, John, I'm so happy for you. I can't believe this is happening."

When John came home that evening, he spoke with his mother.

"Mother, I'm going to join the military."

"No John!" She yelled, "You'll be damned to hell if you take the life of another."

"I'm already damned to hell," John said. "Because of you, I'm a bastard. What do you think the Lord thinks of that?"

"But the Prince, the Prince was your Father."

John interrupted his mother. "Stop it with your stories Mother. The Prince wasn't my Father," said John and then he pointed to James who had now come into the room and said, "and he isn't either. Don't lie to me anymore. I can't take it with your lies."

Adelaide ran to John and hugged him as she began crying.

"Ask then John. Ask why you were picked for the military. Ask if mother's stories were true."

John was getting madder by the moment and began gathering up some of his possessions.

His mother started shouting.

"If you leave if you join the army, don't come back. I don't have a son anymore. I will disown you!"

Although sad to leave his sister, John was glad to be rid of his past. He embraced the opportunity to get away from his mother. He hated the way that his mother, who was already forty years old, carried on with her cousin James who was only twenty-six. They used to lie to people and the authorities because they had the same last name. They claimed to be married. When they conducted the census, they lied about their ages as well so it wouldn't seem so unusual that Emily was fourteen years James' senior. His mother was always worried about keeping up the appearance of living a righteous life.

When John showed up at the barracks of Buckingham Palace, he was excited and nervous. He didn't know what to expect or why they picked him. He was ushered to one of the officials who read his paper's and then checked his directions.

"You will serve with the Prince's Royal Hussars," announced the man.

"What are your talents boy? What can you do?"

John nervously replied, "I'm good with horses, I can train them, shoe them and slaughter them when necessary." The man only took moments to decide and concluded, "Well, good then, you'll be with the Calvary. I need your birth certificate for our records."

"I haven't got one," replied John, "my mother misplaced it years ago."

"Well, where were you born and what were your parents' names?"

"My mother told me I was born in Brighton, Dec. 3rd 1851. Her name is Emily Adelaide Malthouse. My mother claims Prince Albert was my Father, but she's crazy," added John.

"That's preposterous," the man replied. "Your Mother was probably a poor whore. What do you wish me to write down as your father? Shall I list unknown, or do you want to give me a name?"

"You decide," replied John with disgust.

Prince Albert Edward, or Bertie as they called him, presided over the Calvary. The man told Bertie of this ridiculous story of John's parentage, and they both had a good laugh. However, the man was left wondering why John went into the Royal Hussars in the first place. So, Bertie had the man send a letter that stated John had previously served with the Royal Sussex Light Infantry Militia from 11th April 1868 and hoped the man wouldn't think of it anymore. Bertie also knew he should do something about John, so he told John:

"Your mother was my nanny when I was a small boy. I liked your mother and felt I should repay her for her favours to me. That's why I have sent for you. My father, however, was not your father, and I don't want you ever to repeat that. You can tell people you grew up in Brighton and were raised by Quakers and they disowned you when you decided to join the military. That's much more acceptable a stature than to admit you're a bastard son of an east end whore. We will make your paperwork reflect as such. And don't repeat that story. It will bring nothing to you but ridicule. You are now a soldier. You are to be respected and proud. You are in the finest regiment in the world, and you will act as such."

John received the most exceptional training at the Barracks of St Mary's Northgate in Canterbury. Points of lethal inflictions were taught in classes and demonstrated in the field. John's abilities flourished. He became the silversmith and made many of the weapons for the troops. He quickly became the best swordsman and the best shot in the regiment. His ability to communicate with the horses or be a 'horse whisperer' further helped him become the veterinarian's assistant and the lead trainer.

Now it was time for the final test. They ordered him to torture and kill a man as the ultimate test. John did not want to take the life of an innocent man. Bertie had John locked up from September 14th to October 11th, 1871. John refused and finally, Bertie gave in and released him. From that point forward John never looked back.

resemblance between him and John. As John headed up the mountains of the Himalayas, he passed a hill of bleached white bones. They were English men from thirty years ago, the remains of an un-won war. But England needed Afghanistan as a strategic point to suppress the expansion of the Soviet socialist movement. John focused his mind as he prepared for the charge.

John, however, wasn't even wounded. He turned out to be the fiercest soldier of all. He was a one-man fighting machine. He was leaving a trail of decapitated corpses in the path of his stallion. And then later, leaving whole families mutilated in their caves without a trace of who did it (he was a ghost rider). The war in Afghanistan was unlike any from the British training. The Muslim tribesmen refused to fight in battlefields at appointed times. The fighting was guerrilla-like. The more you could intimidate your opponents the better your chance of survival.

John was then appointed torturer of choice. He would skin the rag heads alive, or disembowel them and drape their organs about as warnings to the others. Or he would cut their heads off and scatter their limbs. Sometimes he would prop the bodies up and make them hold their heads in their hands on their lap. He made his own knives. The one most gruesome of all the knives he made was named 'The Ripper'. John's fellow troops would capture their victims and then terrorize them with stories of his torture.

They would say, "Wait until the ripper arrives." And they would hold them down while John ripped their bodies apart alive so their screams would echo throughout the mountains. It was a horrible war, one in that England had lost twice

before. But thanks to John, the Afghans quickly surrendered this time.

On March 21th, 1880, John was awarded the Afghan medal and returned to England. He returned a war hero according to his fellow soldiers, those that survived thanks to his heroic tactics. John was out celebrating in a pub with his cohorts in Canterbury. He was at a pub run by the Hopkins family. Anne, the daughter, was twenty-two and never married. As pitcher after pitcher of beer came to the table, the soldiers were getting loose-lipped. They had been cheering John and welcoming him home after all these years.

They told the ones that hadn't gone to Afghanistan the tales of his fighting abilities. At one point, a cheer was made in John's honour in which they referred to him as 'the Ripper'. One of the soldiers grabbed up Anne, the unmarried beautiful twenty-two-year-old daughter who had been serving them the ale. He turned to John and said, "Here you go, John, it's about time you had a woman. This one comes from good stock. I've known all her family for years. The Howlands and the Hopkins are good folks. Why don't you show this little filly out back and show her the world?"

Anne blushed with embarrassment however she had been mostly taken up with the tales of John and his dashing good looks.

John made frequent trips to the pub while stationed there in Canterbury. He and Anne Francis Hopkins fell in love and were soon married at the Parrish Church of St Paul's on October 20th, 1883. Anne gave birth to a baby boy in March of 1884. The happy couple named the boy John Richard Malthouse. However, the boy died soon after birth. It was difficult for the newlyweds to bury their firstborn son. But that

pain was quickly forgotten as Anne became pregnant again. She gave birth on September 7th, 1885 in Aldershot, Hampshire(where John was deployed) to a healthy baby girl. They named her after her mother, her grandmother and her great-grandmother – Annie Elizabeth Sarah Malthouse.

Chapter 6

Entangled with Royalty

The troops went to York, and Anne gave birth to two more sons that died. One in June of 1887 and one in March of 1888, then Anne was pregnant yet again. Both John and Anne were becoming depressed. John was in the stable one day when he overheard a conversation between Prince Bertie, Lord Arthur Somerset and the young Duke Albert Victor. Lord Arthur Somerset was the head of the stables. Prince Bertie was now forty-one years old, and his son, Duke Albert, or "Eddie" as he called him, was twenty-four years old.

"Arthur," Bertie summoned.

"Yes, what is it your highness," replied Arthur with a lisp. Arthur was a stocky man with flaming carrot red hair, a big bushy moustache and sideburns. He wore a tight leotard riding outfit in shades of beige with a brown felt deer hunter's hat and carried a pair of brown leather gloves and held his riding crop in his left hand between his bent arm and his blazer. He was very flamboyant in character and behaviour.

"Arthur, I want you to meet my son, Eddie. It seems as though Eddie can't handle the stress of student life at Cambridge. He always seems to find himself under the drink or the sheets."

"Oooooooo," giggled Arthur,

"Shame on you," he continued. "Eddie's going to be taking over the troops. I want you to teach him how to ride."

Just then the horse that John was grooming whinnied and the three of them turned and saw John in the horse stall. Bertie said, "Come out here John. Here is my son, Eddie. I want you to teach him how to shoot and lance as good as yourself."

"Yes sir," replied John as he stood erect and saluted Eddie. Bertie put his arm on his son's shoulder and turned him and they walked away.

Meanwhile, John was left standing beside Arthur. Arthur said, "I can't wait to teach that boy how to ride while biting the tips of his right-hand fingernails."

As Bertie and Eddie walked away, Eddie asked his father, "Who is that John fellow? Tell me more about him? He sure is good looking."

Bertie snapped at Eddie, "You think so because he looks just like you."

Eddie replied, "Come to think of it he does look a lot like me, maybe that's why I'm so attracted to him."

Disgusted Bertie blurted out, "Don't even think of it, he's your half-uncle."

"What," questioned Eddie, "how?"

Bertie then said, "His Mother was my nanny, a lovely smart young lady. And my father, Prince Albert got her pregnant two times. She had a daughter, Adelaide and a son, John."

Eddie questioned, "Where is she now?"

Bertie replied, "She died a long time ago, back in 1873. They buried her there at the St George Hanover Square pauper's cemetery. That's where they put her there at the workhouse when she tried to bribe us for support. That's the same thing we had to do with your Annie Crook when you knocked her up. They always go insane when you do that to them. You take away all their nice clothes and cut their hair and tell the staff they are east end whores. When nobody believes their stories, they go insane. Now keep your woody in your pants where it belongs."

Arthur began his training with Eddie on equestrian skills. John used to shake his head at the way Arthur carried on. When John was alone with Eddie, he tried to teach him how to communicate or whisper to the horses and how to fight with a sword and shoot. But Eddie was pathetic at all three skills.

Because Bertie had always resented John and had all but tried to have him killed, John disliked Bertie. But Eddie held no grudges against John; he looked up to John as sort of a familiar companion. He understood he could never say anything to John about being his half-nephew, or it might endanger John's life. Eddie was also becoming very close with Arthur, as they quickly found that they had something in common. They both preferred young boys as opposed to women. Eddie had been matched up by Queen Victoria with an artist named Walter Sickert. He did impressionistic paintings similar to that of Degas. Eddie preferred to paint and indulge in more cultured activities in life as opposed to the military.

One day, Eddie approached John and said, "We're going to London this weekend. I go there frequently to paint under the counsel of an artist. However, Lord Somerset and I often make a pit stop at this wonderful little house on Cleveland Street. They have boys there that can make your eyes cross," and he laughed.

John quickly had a flashback of himself when he was a young boy and abused by the Minister. To reassert himself and his masculinity he quickly replied, “I don’t care much for boys; I prefer a mature woman.”

Eddie was taken aback for a minute; then he came up with an idea.

“I’ll have the artist, Walter, get a model. He has his studio there that he rents out to paint them. You’ll have plenty of privacy.”

John thought for a while. He had had three sons in five years of marriage die. His wife was always either pregnant or grieving over the loss of another child. She was rarely in the mood, and he was becoming sexually frustrated. But the thought of having sex with a boy was unbearable; it would bring back too many memories of his childhood.

“I’ll take you up on the woman,” John replied.

That weekend John told his wife he had to escort the Duke to London for an event. They took a train into London and then they rode their horses to Cleveland Street. Eddie had loaned some clothes to John. He wore dark pants, a vest buttoned up with a white shirt and a high neck collar and ruffles. Eddie warned John that they all took on fake names so as not to alert anyone as to their whereabouts.

When they arrived at the house, Mr Hammond greeted them.

“Hello, Phillip and Charles, I’m sure you’ll be most pleased with the boys tonight.

“And who is this?” asked Mr Hammond as he pushed his way past Eddie and Arthur. John extended his hand and shook it with Mr Hammond.

"I'm um Jack," he said quickly, "that's my name. I'm Jack." Arthur and Eddie looked at each other and Eddie whispered, "I'm um Jack. That was pure genius, don't you think?"

Mr Hammond continued to talk to John.

"Well, Jack I understand Mr Sickert has arranged for a woman, that must be for you. What can a woman do for you that my boys can't? They can do more. And you're not going to catch anything from them like from those filthy whores."

John sternly replied, "I don't want a boy, okay?"

Mr Hammond made a sour-puss face and then held out a key on a small piece of twine.

"Very well," he said, "your bride is waiting over there." He pointed diagonally across the street. John turned to Eddie and said, "What do I do?"

Eddie replied while trying to stifle his speech, "Pick up the brushes and put some paint on the canvas. Hide the picture from her; she won't know any better, then you can fuck her. They know that's why we're paying them. Everybody's a whore the big question is how much money."

Then Phillip (Eddie) and Charles (Arthur) were escorted down the hall. John turned and walked across the street. He opened the door with a little difficulty; he couldn't get the key into the hole as his hands were shaking too much. When he opened the door, candles lit the room. He immediately focused on her. She had fallen asleep waiting for him. She was lying naked on the bed; she looked like an angel John thought. Her skin was beautiful and flaxen white, her hair the colour of gold; it was long and shiny and beautiful. She fell asleep on her left side – this exaggerated the curvature of her body. Her breasts were full and round. As John saw her lying there, he had a flashback to his childhood. The earliest memory of his mother. He was three years old, and his mother was twenty-five, about the same age as this lady: the same coloured beautiful hair and the same skin. His mother used to be beautiful. He sat down behind the aisle, still mesmerised by her beauty. He picked up a brush and began making strokes. He had never painted before; the brush strokes were large and deliberate with little resemblance to the scene in front of him. The colours were off, and the mixtures were all muddied. His model did not wake up, so John continued to paint.

Chapter 7
The Royal Rape

After about an hour and a half, there was a knock on the door. When John opened it, it was Eddie. The arrival had also awakened the woman who sat upright. Eddie asked laughingly as he came right in and examined John's painting.

"What are you doing? I paid for you to pop her, not paint her?"

"But she was asleep," responded John defensively.

"Well, then wake her up," replied Eddie, as he walked over and stood beside the woman.

"Look, she's awake now. Now you can do her. Or better yet we both will."

Eddie started pulling down his pants. John began to have flashbacks and pictured his mother and her stories of being with Prince Albert. Ever since the Afghan war, John suffered from these visions from time to time. He was immobilised, even though he was watching, he wasn't able to do anything. The girl was protesting which seemed to excite Eddie even more. Then Eddie flipped the woman over onto her hands and knees, and he drove himself into her, he gave her every bit of his manhood. John stood immobilised watching the woman's face as her eyes silently pleaded with him to do something. It was over within minutes. Eddie pulled back up his pants and walked over and shook John, "Come on, wake up, let's go."

When John rode back on the train, the events seemed like a dream to him. They didn't seem real.

The next day, Walter Sickert went into the studio and was fascinated by the painting. It was hauntingly beautiful, and he loved it. Then the woman came knocking at the door. When Walter answered it, the woman put her fist on the door and demanded to know who the man was last night. Walter didn't want to tell her, but she threatened him. She was tough and intimidating. She grabbed him by the hair and threatened to punch him.

Walter relented, "It was the Duke, Duke Albert or Eddie as they call him. But you better keep your mouth shut, or you'll end up like Annie, the last one who threatened him. She's at Marylebone house now. They say she's gone insane."

"Annie who?" The woman demanded as she pulled his hair harder.

"Annie Crook," he said, "You'll wind up just like her, don't say a word. Do you understand? You should be afraid of him."

When she left him, he muttered, "Stupid damn whores."

Mary, however, was a poor desperate soul whose life had turned out for the worse. She lived on hand to mouth handouts by her boyfriend who gave her food and shelter in exchange for sex. So, Mary waited for the appropriate amount of time and then sent a letter which she wrote herself as she didn't want anyone to know what she was doing.

August 4th, 1888, a letter was presented to Queen Victoria by the Prime Minister Robert Cecil, the Marquis of Salisbury.

Dear Queen Victoria,

I no wat hapnd to Ane Cruck she was mi frend and im not goin to let the sam thin hapn to me. Yor lovely grandson Duke Eddie rapd me wen i was supos to be modlin for his pantin me and im pregnant now. Iv got 1 ov his silver butins. Iv told ol mi frens so dont thinc u cin do awa with me. Be cuz thel ol tel the trooth. I want mone to suport the child and miself. I xpect an anser in a timle fashon.

Yours trule Mary 27 Dorset St Spitalfields.

"What shall we do?" asked Queen Victoria, "it seems as though we can't keep Eddie's nose out of trouble."

The Prime Minister replied, "It's not his nose that's getting him into trouble. This is not going to be as easy as the others. I'll talk with Bertie first about his son's whereabouts. I suspect there's probably some truth to this," said Mr Cecil, "This is not the sort of thing we want getting out to the press, not at this time in England, we're already on the verge of a social uprising."

"Make it go away then," said Victoria. "I'll send this Mary out a letter immediately telling her we are investigating the matter. I'll let her know we've notified the head of my regiment in Sussex. I'll pretend they are in charge of the investigation. I'll be very vague as to what they are supposed to be investigating. Meanwhile, we will conduct our little search."

The Prime Minister questioned Bertie, and then Bertie talked with his son. When Bertie came into Eddie's room, he had been lying down on a chaise.

Bertie yelled at Eddie, “Eddie, it seems you can’t keep your pecker out of trouble. You got another whore pregnant, and she’s trying to blackmail us. Who is she?”

Eddie replied: “I don’t know. What are you talking about?”

“She claims she was supposed to be a model and you raped her,” demanded Bertie.

“Oh, that one. That one was supposed to be John’s, and I didn’t rape her, she loved it,” smirked Eddie.

“Who was she?” Bertie demanded.

“I don’t know, I barely remember. I had a good drunk going on and then some,” laughed Eddie.

“Why don’t you clean it up just like that Annie girl?” Bertie then replied as he grabbed the front of Eddie’s shirt with his hand, “Because she took one of your buttons! I thought you were sticking to boys?”

Eddie jumped up off the chaise and said, “Yeah, well, this thing has a mind of its own,” he laughed while he grabbed his crotch and pretended it was pulling him around the room.

“This is not funny!” Bertie shouted. Eddie then nonchalantly replied, “Oh, she’s probably lying. I don’t think Annie knew who the father was either. These girls blame it on me so they can get paid better. They’re all just whores. Why don’t you pay her off?” replied Eddie.

Then Bertie walked up closer to Eddie and asked while staring into his eyes.

“Aren’t you worried about catching some God, awful disease from one of them?”

Eddie again casually replied, “Oh you hadn’t heard? I already have. One of those fucking whores gave me syphilis. I figured Dr Gull already told you by now. Look at this,” he said while holding out his hands, they were quivering slightly. "This is why I'm no damn good at shooting. It's in my nerves already and going to my head soon, I'm sure."

Bertie turned red with rage.

"God damn them, Eddie, I didn't know," then he became tearful while embracing his son. He sobbed to Eddie, "I'll figure out who this whore was and I'll have her heart cut out!"

"Stop crying, Father; it was just a matter of time, I've had it for a while now. I can deal with it," reassured Eddie.

Bertie continued, "Well, I can't deal with it. You were to be the King of England after me. How can I find this whore?"

"Ask John, he painted her," replied Eddie.

Bertie summoned John from York. It was the bank holiday weekend. Bertie asked John if he remembered what this woman, Mary, looked like. John vaguely did. He got orders to question around Whitechapel. See if anyone knows anything. He told him that if he found the woman, he wanted her 'heart cut out'.

Chapter 8

The Hunt Is On

It was a bank holiday weekend. Eddie said he would love to come with John and hunt for the woman, but he was laid up in bed with a bad case of gout and could barely walk across the room. So, John's superior went with him. John kissed his pregnant wife, Anne, goodbye and set off to London. They went immediately to the return address written on the letter by Mary. It was a store on the first floor of an area mixed with shops and doss housing. They looked around and decided to stay at the Crossingham's Lodging House there across Dorset Street where a lot of other soldiers frequented the place; they would blend right in.

Saturday, the first day there, John thought he recognised Mary, the woman that he had painted. The woman that reminded him so much of his mother. She was just as beautiful by day as she was that night thought John. But he couldn't tell for sure as everyone looks different when they are naked and horizontal. He watched her and noticed her talking with a lady who was staying at their Crossingham's. They decided to buddy up with the other lady and see if she knew anything.

They followed the lady on Monday night, the night of the holiday's big celebration. Whitechapel was a filthy hideous place. Most of the people survived on gin to blur the existence of their miserable lives. Many of the immigrants including the Jews and the Irish were forced to live there because of cultural discrimination. They attempted to make a living. This, in turn, made it even harder on the native English folk to make an honest living. So many of the indigenous English people turned to a life of corruption. Their souls had died. They were the living dead. They walked the streets with empty blank stares. They would startle visitors when they blinked. It was the only indicator that they were not dead. The animals ready for slaughter were herded through the cobbled streets, their excrement never removed. Every woman there could be coerced into prostitution to make enough money to eat. Even if they tried to sell matches or other trivial things, they couldn't make a living. The going rate was three pennies for an upright. That meant three pennies to do it in an alley standing up. No one dared to lie down on the ground for the filth, and the stench would have been too much to bear. The women didn't wear underwear under their layers upon layers of clothing. Most of them wore everything they owned for they never knew which doss house they could get into for the night, if any at all. The doss houses wouldn't let the women bring their John's back to bed with them. Most of the women would make enough for their doss and then lose it again to a glass of gin thus creating a cycle of destruction. They were forced to turn as many tricks as they could. But with each trick, they had to try to size up the man as to whether he was going to pay them, or maybe he'd try to steal from them. Or perhaps they'd catch a disease from the man.

There were gangs of Irish immigrants that would force the women into paying them so-called 'protection money' (against the clients). The lucky ones worked in the brothels, but they were more attractive and younger than the streetwalkers. The streets at night were dark and had only a few lit gas lamps per lane. The houses were cramped and filled with two or three families sharing a flat. Typhoid, tuberculosis, syphilis and gonorrhea were rampant, and so were the afflictions of alcoholism, pancreatitis, liver cirrhosis and more. Rats were at appalling levels, and the dead were left in houses for days before arrangements could be made by the state to fetch the corpses. The air wreaked of death.

Whitechapel residents were the scum of the earth, and they were being swept under the carpet by the British aristocracy. They were contained nice and neatly in one corner of the city. Prince Albert, Victoria's husband, used to argue that wealth was an accident of society and that all children should have an adequate chance to survival, but the parliament wouldn't hear of his suggestions, they were too caught up with their greed.

John grew up there in that armpit, so it wasn't a shock to him. John and his superior followed the woman into a pub. The pub was called the Two Brewers Public House. John's friend quickly started chatting her up. Her name as she told them was Pearly Poll. One of Pearly Poll's friends rapidly joined the threesome, as she saw an opportunity for a possible trick. Pearly Poll introduced her as Emma. As John had lied before back at the Cleveland Street brothel, John gave his name once again as 'Jack'. His friend and Pearly Poll did most of the talking. The women felt lucky to have potentially landed soldiers, as they were the best catch. They were reliable and safe.

The women went on a pub crawl with the soldiers believing that that would be the only trick they would have to turn for the night. The area was alive with bonfires and other various sorts of celebrations of the holiday. After John had had a few under his belt, he suggested going to the White Swan. So, Pearly Poll asked him how he knew about the White Swan, and he told her he used to live around there when he was a boy. Pearly Poll asked where and he said Buck's Row. His friend thought he was doing too much talking and not enough questioning, so he hushed John up by jabbing him in the leg. John reoriented himself as to why they were there, and let the conversation drop. Neither one of the women appeared to know anything about Mary or Prince Albert Victor.

Chapter 9

The 'First Kill' in London

John's friend suggested they take a walk outside. Once outside he motioned to John by putting his right finger in and out of a hole he made with his left finger and thumb. Then he pointed at a dark alley named George Court. His friend and Pearly Poll broke off, and it left John alone with Emma. Emma quickly took him over to a corner. John was 5'7" and a half, but Emma was much shorter. John led Emma over to the landing of the building there and put her up on the first step, so he was just the right height, he didn't have to bend his legs. He turned her around and entered her from the back, so he didn't have to face her. Then John began giving Emma the sexual workout of her life; however, his mind was not focused on the sex. He was having flashbacks about telling Pearly Poll he used to live on Buck's Row with his mother's Hosiers there. He was now plying his trade for 'God and Country' in an attempt to scare off any prostitutes from blackmailing randy male British royalty for impregnating them. All this to keep the Queen and the Kingdom appear squeaky clean and moral. He knew he was going to kill this woman. When Emma tried to snap him out of his thoughts and said, "If you're going to keep this up I'm going to have to charge you more. Get it off already you are killing me."

That was the trigger he needed; he grabbed his bayonet from his leg strap with his right hand, reached around her and stabbed her right through her sternum and into her heart — almost sudden death. Then John, being completely in control as a trained killer, knew the bayonet wound would immediately identify him as a soldier and he was not about to hang for killing this whore. So, he laid her body down and took out his pocket knife and began stabbing at her spleen and liver. But then his thoughts turned more to his whore mother, and he jabbed at her breasts and groin.

He stabbed her with the pocket knife one time for each miserable year he was alive. Counting in his head as he did: *1,2,3,4,5,6,7,8,9,10,11,12,13,14,15,16,17,18,19,20,21,22,23, 24,25,26,27,28,29,30,31,32,33,34,35,36,37 and one for good luck; 38.*

John then wiped the blood off his hands with Emma's dress, pulled himself together and met up with his friend the superior, the corporal who had been patiently waiting for him. John didn't mention a word to him about killing Emma as they walked back to Crossingham's Lodge.

The sad irony of it was that he himself was the bastard son of such a royal liaison, but his mother was not a whore. She was a beautiful 18-year-old Quaker from a wealthy family. She was unknowingly groomed for seduction for the years she tutored the children of Prince Albert and Queen Victoria. However, the Royals would never let him know the truth about his bloodline as he was now the 'Royal Assassin'. John had been trained in all methods of killing, he even trained with the Gurkhas in Afghanistan and the Indian Commandos on silent kills using a dull knife to sever the vocal chords. John was resourceful and could use whatever it would take to kill. But the knives would now be his modus operandi. Thus, sending out a message, they would all be from the same killer.

Pearly Poll, however, had been waiting out in the shadows and when she saw the soldiers leave she went looking for Emma. She found Emma lying in a pool of blood with her eyes still wide open. Pearly Poll let out a small scream, "Murder," and then quickly hushed her mouth as she knew who had done it. Pearly Poll didn't know where to go, and she couldn't go back to Crossingham's where she had been staying because that's where they were staying, that's what the corporal told her. And she thought surely 'Jack' as he told her his name was, would kill her too. Pearly Poll ran the other direction crying and confused. She was hurrying up Flower and Dean Street when she heard a voice calling to her, "Pearly Poll, is that you?"

And the figure came closer. Pearly Poll recognised the person to be one of her friends, so she called out to her, "Polly, it's me, Pearly Poll, and I'm in terrible danger. Can I stay the night with you?" Polly took Pearly Poll to Thrawl Street to a house where she had been living with four other women. It was already four o'clock in the morning, so Pearly Poll and Polly stayed up, and Pearly Poll told Polly all about what had happened. Including the fact that the soldier's name was Jack and that he had grown up on Buck's Row. Polly suggested Pearly Poll hideout as she said, he will be out to get her. Polly told Pearly Poll she couldn't stay with her as the other women wouldn't allow it. So, Pearly Poll left in the morning and stayed out with a cousin in a flat on Drury Lane.

John, however, had gone back to Crossingham's that night and was waiting for Pearly Poll to return. After an hour or so, when she didn't come back, John became suspicious. He couldn't go out and do too much asking around for fear that the body would soon be discovered and that he might be exposed. John returned to York on the early morning train. He tried to carry on at the Barracks there in York as though nothing happened. Anne, his five-month pregnant wife, had noticed some unusual behaviour in him.

Emma's body had been identified as that of Martha Tabram by her former husband. He said they separated thirteen years ago. He said Martha was about forty years old. Pearly Poll whose real name was Mary Ann Connolly had notified the police, and there were already line-ups in progress at the Tower of London and Wellington Barracks.

Detective Edmond Reid of the H Division Metropolitan Police oversaw many of the events. Including encouraging Pearly Poll to be very careful about what she says because she might still be in danger. The two guards she picked out of the line-up had rock-solid alibis. She was dismissed as a poor witness, which they surmised was due to her drunkenness at the time. One detective, however, did focus on the fact that she claimed the soldier said he lived on Buck's Row. That was about the only useful information that they got out of her.

Back at the Barracks in York on Tuesday, August 7th, John met up with Eddie who was still whining in bed about his gout. Eddie was laughing and turned to John and said:

"I thought you were supposed to question them, not kill them? Did you fuck her to death? Is that what happened?" laughed the Duke.

"She reminded me of my mother" responded John.

"You loved your mother that much?" sarcastically teased the Duke. John did not respond. Then the Duke remembered his conversation with his father about John's mother being the nanny and mistress to his grandfather Prince Albert, Victoria's late husband. Eddie didn't say any more about John's mother.

About a week and a half later, John went back in to see Eddie. Eddie's doctor the royal physician Dr Gull was examining Eddie's gout which was showing no sign of improvement. John was about to turn and leave when instead Eddie asked him to stay and introduced him to Dr Gull John then confessed to Dr Gull that he had developed a sore on his penis. Dr Gull asked to examine it. When John pulled down his pants, and Dr Gull saw a sizeable red chancre he then questioned John about his recent activities. John confessed to the use of a prostitute about ten days ago. Dr Gull regretfully informed John that he had contracted syphilis.

Eddie jumped into the conversation and said, "Look this is what you have to look forward to," he held out his quivering hands. Then Dr Gull told John of what he was to expect in the future.

"The sore will go away soon. Then in about three to six weeks you will be covered with a rash, you will have headaches and fever, you'll be tired and your throat will hurt, some of your hair might fall out and your glands will swell from the infection. It's possible you'll have seizures or a stroke, but if you're lucky, all of that will go away. Then maybe years later it will damage your heart or your nerves or go to your eyes or your bones and joints. These whores should all rot in hell for what they have done. They're filthy despicable vermin that spread more diseases than rats. They should all be rounded up and extinguished!"

John's life flashed before him. John was a soldier, fighting hand to hand combat for all those years and never even sustained a nick and now this. A whore was going to be the death of him.

Dr Gull questioned John further, "Tell me more about yourself, do you have any children?"

"I have one daughter and three sons that have died."

Dr Gull quickly responded, "Three sons, that died; tell me about your mother?"

"She was a whore!" interjected Eddie.

Dr Gull turned and looked at Eddie and then turned back around to John and said, "Is this true? Was your mother a whore?"

John didn't respond.

Dr Gull then continued, "If it's true, your mother was a whore, and you were a bastard son; that would explain why all of your son's keep dying. It is bad genes. Your mother has damned you for her sins."

"Eddie," said the doctor, "see to it that John joins our brotherhood and receives the teachings of our Lord. I wish for him to become a freemason. Maybe his mother's sins can be avenged."

At the first freemasons meeting, they talked about King Solomon's Temple and the traitors and the transgressions against the Jews. They also discussed that Sir Charles Warren, the head of the London Police department was soon to be made the First Master Mason of the Quatuor Coronati Lodge 2076. After the meeting, the Prime Minister spoke with Sir Charles Warren. They talked for a while, and the conversation ended with the Prime Minister wanting to be kept apprised of the developments of the murder case that was reported to be a soldier. The Prime Minister then had a talk with Eddie about minding his randy desires.

Chapter 10

The Search for the Killer

The search for the soldier who committed the murder was heating up. John knew he had to find Pearly Poll and shut her up. He had found, through casual inquest of the police department, that Pearly Poll was possibly too scared to identify him, however, he also found that she spent the first night at a house on Thrawl Street. John needed to go back to London and see if she told anyone else about him, he also needed to continue to check into the friends of Mary and her supposed pregnancy. He had a lot on his mind.

Thursday, Aug 30th, Eddie took off for the Danby Lodge in Grosmont, Yorkshire to stay with the Viscount Downe. John told his wife he would be accompanying the Prince. However, he caught the train into London. He checked into an ordinary lodging house on Flower and Dean Street. This was probably one of the roughest streets of all; it was nicknamed 'Hell's Street'.

John dressed in plain clothes and went over to the house of Mrs Holland on Thrawl Street and began casually questioning around; he quickly found that Pearly Poll must have been the guest of Polly because she was the only woman of the four who was living there that was missing. None of the others seemed to know anything of substance. Mrs Holland said Polly hadn't been there for the last ten days.

John traced her to the workhouse on Prince's Street. He quickly caught up with her. John was a natural tracker. Nothing went unnoticed by John. He was following her up Osborn Street and then approached her when she got to the intersection of White Chapel Road. He began to walk eastward with her as they talked. Polly was somewhat pretty. However, she had many missing teeth and she was very drunk. She was loose-lipped, and just what John wanted. He asked her about Pearly Poll. She told him about Poll thinking it was a soldier from Buck's Row. John played dumb and asked Polly to show him where Buck's Row was, John knew the general direction, and it wouldn't take long to get there.

He started chatting her up.

"What's your real name, I know it's not Polly?" asked John as he walked with his arm around her giving her support.

"My father named me Mary, but I never use it," replied Polly.

"Mary's a lovely name. Can I call you Mary?" asked John. John quickly thought about the Mary who claimed to be pregnant.

"Mary, you're not pregnant, are you?"

"Oh no," she laughed, "I'm not pregnant."

"What would you do if you were pregnant?" asked John.

"Miss Emily would take care of that. She takes care of all of us that get pregnant. She can sew our 'what knots' back together, so we get paid extra for being a virgin. Also, she can do abortions on those of us that get pregnant."

"Who is Mrs Emily?" John quickly asked.

"Oh, that's Mrs Holland, I call her Mrs Emily, that's her first name. The lady I had that gave me an abortion before Mrs Emily gave me an infection. I got laid up in Hanover Square and just about died from it. I think the doctor, Dr Williams or Fenton did something to me. Because I've never been pregnant since."

John began having flashbacks. He had visions of the sign outside Hanover Square Workhouse where he had spent much of his troubled youth. Then he was thinking about his mother again. And the fact that this Mrs Holland's first name was Emily. Could she be his mother? Could Emily be his mother that had remarried someone else? They reached Buck's Row. It looked different from how he had remembered it as a teenager. A couple of the cottages that were beside his mother's Hosiers had been knocked down, and a railway track led through the alley between Malt House Cottage and the stables where he used to work. He brought Polly through the stable entrance and stood across the alley from his mother's old place. It still had the old weathered sign, Malt House Cottage, on the door. John was fighting terrible flashbacks at this time. They appeared like a rapid succession of photographs in his head. John held Polly's face toward the direction of the Malt House cottage.

"Do you know what place this is? Do you know who lives here?"

"I don't know who lives here?" replied Polly.

"Are you sure you don't? Did Emily used to work here?" asked John.

"Work as what?" asked Polly.

"A dressmaker," said John

“She was a seamstress.” Polly replied “every seamstress I know is now a prostitute just like me. The Jews have put us all out of business.”

John pulled Polly into the shadows and motioned her to be quiet. A man was knocking at the door of Malt House Cottage. Another man opened the door, and they began to talk.

“Mr Tipple we made a good turnout tonight. Those ladies pulled in two pounds each.”

They talked a little longer while appearing to be splitting up the profit money and then the men left. John realised his mother’s Hosiers had turned into a brothel. He couldn’t control the thoughts in his head any longer. He pictured his cousin James as his mother’s pimp. His mother was a whore, and she just called herself a seamstress as half the other whores do when claiming their vocation. His mind was racing. Was she a whore all along? Had he ever really seen her make clothes? Had she forced his sister Adelaide into being a whore too? He was probably blind to it all that time. All those stories about his dad being the Prince; she probably had no idea who his father was. That’s why all his sons were dead.

John then watched his hands reach out and strangle Polly as the train went by. He could only think about how much he hated his mother. John cut Polly’s stomach open and disembowelled her as he did in Afghanistan. He cut her tongue in half as a warning to Pearly Poll to keep her mouth shut. Then came a flashback of her, saying her name was Mary. He doubted if she would tell the truth if she were pregnant, so he cut out her womb and took off her apron and wrapped the organ in it. He heard some people coming and he quickly ran down the alley. He passed two of the slaughtermen and told them there was a murder in the alley; then he hid in one of the horse stalls. He communicated to the horses to be quiet. And from the horse stall, he listened to the commotion. It was about four o'clock in the morning. The police and a doctor who came had her body sent to the Whitechapel Workhouse Infirmary. John just disappeared into the crowd in the morning. It wasn't unusual for someone to be walking down Buck's Row with blood on their hands as it was a frequent sight so close to the slaughtering yards. He washed off his hands in a public fountain and went back to his room on Flower and Dean Street.

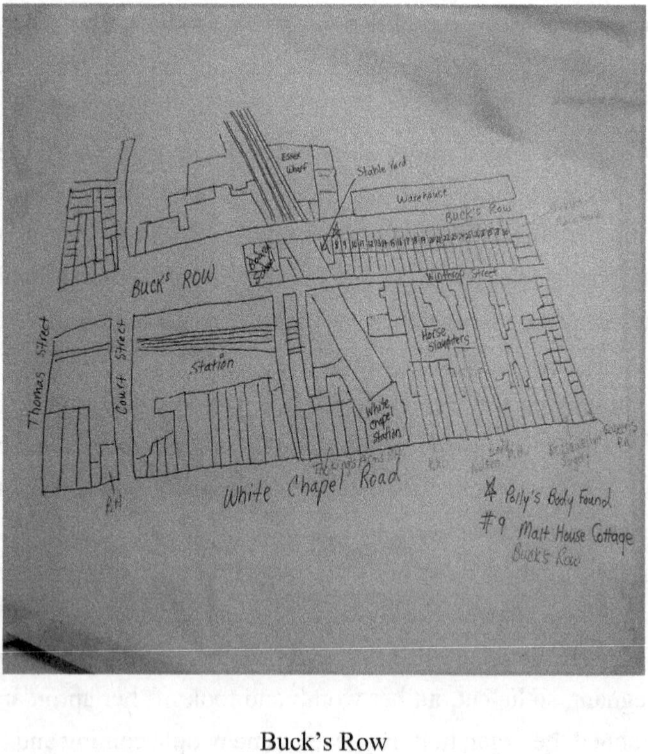

Buck's Row

Later that afternoon, he went over to the Whitechapel infirmary dressed in the beautiful clothes that Prince Eddie had loaned him for the Cleveland Street expedition. He claimed he was Dr Williams, and that he wanted to examine the body. His instincts were now kicking in, with the urge to see the carcass, to see his kill. He took a quick peek at her and then asked Mr Mann, the keeper of the mortuary, who would be the assigned doctor to the case. Mr Mann informed him that Dr Llewellyn had already conducted the post-mortem. John asked the man about his findings, but the man was ignorant. As John was leaving his sister, Adelaide saw him. She hadn't seen John since he stormed out of their mother's house nineteen years ago. But she recognised him.

She yelled, "John," and he turned and saw her; then realising that he couldn't ruin his cover, he turned back around and kept walking out. Adelaide quickly asked Mr Mann about him, and Roger Mann told Adelaide that he was Dr Williams. Adelaide was there because she had fallen into terrible poverty after the death of her mother. She had been hopping from workhouse to workhouse, working as a nurse trying to survive. Adelaide was very suspicious of her brother's appearance at the morgue. She wondered why he claimed to be Dr Williams.

John went back to York that afternoon on the train. The Duke hadn't returned from Yorkshire. So, John put the womb in a pail of beer to keep it preserved. Duke Eddie returned to the Barracks on Friday, September 7th. Lord Salisbury was in Eddie's room, to hear all the details of the trip. When John came in, he came in with the womb in the pail of beer, covered with a rag.

John exclaimed, "I've got one for you to check out. Her name was Mary."

He had always maintained his somewhat formal military posture and behaviour toward Duke Eddie, who was both his commander in chief and royalty. John was sworn to protect Eddie with his life. John held out the pail toward Eddie's hand. Eddie turned and looked at Arthur with an inquisitive expression.

"What do you have in there, her head?" laughed Eddie, "I heard you killed another one."

John replied formally, "This is her womb," as he held it up with his other hand. Eddie and Arthur curled up their legs and bent away and laughed.

Arthur asked, "What do you want us to do with it?"

John replied, "I thought you could have your doctor, Dr Gull check it and see if she was pregnant. Can't he do that?"

Then Eddie looked confused and asked John, "I thought you used to help out the veterinarians?"

"Yes," replied John, "but we never had to see if one of them were pregnant, we only use to spay them. I wouldn't know what it would look like if it were under my nose."

Eddie then asked, "I was sent a message from Dr Gull that someone was looking at the corpse claiming to be Dr Williams, but he wasn't there in London. Do you know anything about that?"

John snickered a little bit, "I wanted to take a peek at her. I thought it was a safe thing to claim."

"Listen, 'Doctor Williams'," Eddie said "we have summoned for the real doctor Williams to come and do a clinic in Whitechapel tomorrow. Then it won't be questioned that he wasn't around at the time. I like the idea about you being a doctor. I find that pretty funny. Go ahead and pretend to be a doctor. They're going to blame your last murder on this Jewish man who walks around in a leather apron all the time threatening the whores with a knife. I had a chat with the prime minister who spoke with the chief of police. We've got a couple in the Criminal Investigation Department (CID) that we can bring to our side by way of the brotherhood of Free Masons, they are sworn to protect the brothers with their lives, just as you have sworn to protect mine. Which reminds me, where's your knife?"

John pulled out a knife strapped to his calf under his pant leg and held it up. It was about nine inches long and very sharp and shiny, it had a jagged edge on the bottom.

"Good Lord," exclaimed Eddie, "What kind of knife is that?"

"I call it the Ripper. I made it myself," John proclaimed proudly. "Remind me not to have you as my doctor after Gull dies," Eddie laughed, and Arthur made a sarcastic terrified face.

Then Eddie continued, "We got a letter today, don't mind me for opening, addressed to John Malthouse from the Christchurch Hospital. The letter was from a nurse there named Adelaide. It read that there were interesting statements made by a patient by the name of Annie Chapman and that you might want to talk with her. Who is this Adelaide?"

"She's my sister," said John.

Eddie looked a little surprised and then continued, "So I did a little checking. I want you to go back to London and find this whore who is getting discharged tomorrow. She's been staying at the Crossinham's. She was yapping at the mouth there at Christchurch, something about a friend getting bribe money from the royalty. Oh, how nice the grapevine grows. I love having connections. You know, those whores never use their real name. This one will be hard to miss though. She's got a black eye. See if she knows anything."

John had received his orders, so he was about to leave the room when Arthur said: "Wait, you can have this for a disguise."

Arthur gave John his brown deerstalker hat. Then John left the room. Arthur was just in heaven, his hands and wrists were flapping like a butterfly, and his lisp was now very exaggerated as he was enjoying all the drama. He began to try to spank Eddie with his riding crop, but Eddie shooed him off.

Chapter 11

Expedition Crossingham's

John made an excuse to his wife, Anne, and then he caught the first train to London. He checked into the Crossingham's again, as that's where Annie had previously stayed. The Crossingham's could hold up to about three hundred people, and he could blend in and question around casually without alarming anyone. He learned that the lady with the black eye went by the name of 'Dark Annie' and that although she hadn't been there for a week, they believed she would be back, as she always came on the weekends to stay with a man she called her pensioner. Sure enough, John was sitting in the public kitchen when he saw a woman come in soon after midnight. She sat down and drank a pitcher of beer with a man she called Fred. She told Fred she was feeling very sick, she reached into her pocket and took out a pillbox and it broke onto the floor. She swallowed down a pill and then looked for something to hold them. She found a corner of an envelope, put the pills into it, folded it over and then headed up to her room.

The deputy saw Annie sneaking up and sent the old night watchman, John Evans up to collect her doss money. Annie didn't have any money, so she was told to leave. She went down to Timothy Donovan's office and pleaded with him. He wouldn't allow it.

He said, "You've got enough money to pay for beer, but you can't pay for your bed. Get out!"

As Annie walked away, she yelled, "Don't let my room go; I'll be back with the money."

Annie then set off toward Stratford, where she usually solicited.

It was now around 1:30 in the morning. John quickly went up to his room and got his black coat and the hat that Arthur had lent to him and headed out on to the street after her. He wanted to get to her as quickly as possible because if she did know anything, he didn't want her telling anyone.

He called to her, "Madame, excuse me, Madame."

Annie stopped and turned around. John held out two polished farthings.

"Did these just fall out of your pocket?" John asked. Seeing the money, Annie quickly thought and then reached into her pocket and pulled out the envelope with the pills. She pretended to act surprised.

"Oh, they're gone! Why yes, they did just fall out of my pocket. Thank you, Sir, you're very kind for letting me know."

Then she put the two farthings and the envelope with the pills back in her pocket.

John quickly said, "That's quite a shiner you have there," as he touched the side of Annie's temple and appeared to examine her black eye.

"I'm a doctor," said John, "you should have that attended to."

"Yes," said Annie. "I've just spent the last week in the infirmary for my lungs. The doctor there already looked at my bruise."

"What's your name?" asked John.

"Dark Annie," she replied.

"I can see why you're called that," joked John, as he studied Annie's appearance. Annie was only five-feet tall, she had brown wavy hair, ashen skin and light blue eyes, accentuated with the bruise around the right one. She was wearing a long black skirt with a dark brown shirt and a black coat. She began laughing and pulled up her skirt for John to see her red and white striped stockings and old worn boots.

When she looked down at her boots, she said, "I've been trying to get enough money to buy myself a pair of new boots. I told my best friend, Amelia, when I get a new pair of boots, I'm going to go out to Kent and do some hop picking. The doctor there told me the fresh air would be good for my lungs."

"Yes, that's correct," said John continuing to pretend to be a doctor also, "I tell my patients to go and get fresh air also. Where about in Kent do you pick the hops?"

"I go out to Hunton near Maidstone."

John then put his arm around Annie and led her down the street.

"Why don't you tell me all about hop picking and we'll see if I can't give you enough money for a new pair of boots," said John.

They didn't go into any bars as Annie said she felt too sick to drink. For a couple of hours, they meandered around the streets. Because Annie wouldn't drink, she didn't become very loose-lipped. John had to be very careful about how he got his information out of Annie.

"You say you were in a hospital? Which one were you in again?"

Dark Annie replied, "Christchurch, that's where I was."

John quickly had a flashback to when he was looking at the body of Polly, when he was pretending to be Dr Williams and then saw his sister there, she was a nurse.

He said, "Yes, I haven't formally introduced myself. I am doctor Williams. Pleased to make your acquaintance." And he turned and bowed to Dark Annie.

"I sometimes work out of the hospital there, and I have a sister that is a nurse. Her name is Adelaide. Do you know her?"

"Oh yes," replied Annie, "she was my nurse at times. She's the best one there. She took excellent care of me."

John quickly worked off his hunch.

"Adelaide told me you were telling everyone about a friend of yours going to collect some money from the queen."

Dark Annie replied, "Oh, I didn't tell everyone, but Adelaide was particularly interested. She kept asking me if it was possible my friend knew who had committed the murders, and wanted reward money."

"Why don't you share your little secret with me?" begged John.

"I guess it won't hurt," said Annie. "I have this friend named Mary; we meet at the Brittania most days, that's where I got this black eye from that horrible woman that's trying to steal my pensioner. Anyway, she came over looking for me one morning. She had a letter in her hand. She's from Ireland and she never learned to read or write well. So, she wanted me to read this letter to her. Usually, she lets her boyfriend, Barnett read to her, but this time she didn't want him to know. I read the letter to her. I don't remember the exact wording, but it had a lot of fancy words about secret detectives investigating allegations before monies would be appropriated and things like that. When I asked her what it was all about, she wouldn't tell me. But I know Mary, she's up to something."

John started getting agitated. He had flashbacks of Mary looking at him while he watched Eddie rape her.

He asked, "When was the letter sent and who sent it?"

"Oh, I don't remember that. It was a while ago," replied Annie.

Then Annie had a thought, "I threw out the envelope, but half of it missed the garbage can and landed on the floor. I left it there, then somebody else must have picked it up and set it on the mantel, and that was the piece I've got in my pocket" she said, and she pulled it out of her pocket. John took it from her and read the post-date 'London August 23rd' , then there was the letter 'M' under that the number '2' and further down an 'Sp' the rest had been ripped off. When he starred at the blue seal, 'Sussex Regiment', it set John off. That's where his mother claimed to have been raised. All those stories about the Prince being his father; he wanted to grab his mother by the throat and make her tell him the truth. He needed to find her.

He turned toward Annie and asked, "Do you know any Emily that lives around here?"

"I know lots of Emilys; my best friend is named Amelia. Who is she and what's her last name?"

"She's a good patient of mine, she would be about the same age as my mother, and I'm not sure what her last name is now as she might have gotten married. But it used to be Malthouse."

Then Dark Annie asked, "Well, how old are you, doctor?"

"I'm thirty-seven," replied John.

Annie thought for a minute and then she said, "I know of an old lady named Emily Richardson; she lives just up here on Hanbury Street."

"Take me there," said John.

Annie walked John down a couple of blocks to a row house.

"This is it," Annie said, as she stood in front of the house.

John began to feel his face becoming blotchy. A fever was coming on. The infection from the syphilis was taking hold. The illness was distorting his capacity to think clearly. He was becoming agitated, but he tried to maintain his calm.

"Tell me about this Emily who lives here?" Annie said.

"I don't know much about her; I hear she takes in people and is very hospitable. There's a whole lot of people that live in there with her, something like seventeen."

John tried to peek in the windows, but he couldn't see inside. Then he went in the backyard through a gate. He was dragging Annie around by the hand. They couldn't see any better in the backyard. So, he brought her back around to the front.

"Go knock on the door," said John.

"No way," said Annie, "it's only about half-past four in the morning."

John saw someone heading toward the gate, and he pulled Annie into the shadow. The man went into the yard for only about two minutes and then came back out again.

"Let's follow him," said John.

Annie was getting dragged all over the place by her hand. They saw the man stop and talk with another man briefly and then hurry on. John stopped and asked the man who he was just talking to. John pretended to be an undercover policeman.

The man said, "Oh, that's John."

John then asked, "Does he live there?" and pointed toward the house on Hanbury Street.

"No," replied the man, "he lives on John Street."

"What was he doing over there then?" asked John.

"His mother lives there," replied the man.

John thanked him, and he took Dark Annie by the hand and walked back to the house.

Annie asked, "What is going on?"

John didn't answer her. His fever was getting much worse. He couldn't stop thinking about Emily there, with a son named John about the same age as him, and who lives on

John Street. John's memories of leaving the John's Street house when his mother disowned him was invading his mind.

He stood in front of the house and leaned Annie up against the shutters.

"You're going to earn your money for those boots now. I want to do it in the backyard. I want to call you mom, and you call me son okay? Will you? Will you do that?"

Annie said, "Yes, I'll call you anything if you just hurry it up already."

John again dragged Annie by the hand through the gate, and into the backyard. John stood Annie up on the landing as she was shorter than he.

He said, "Lift your skirt, Mommy," and Annie said, "Okay, son."

As Annie lifted her skirt, John grabbed her by the throat. He watched her face. He watched her eyes bulge and her tongue swell and protrude. He watched the life drain away from her as he choked her. He thought silently, *I hate you, Mother. I hate you for being the two-faced whore that you are. I hate you for only caring about yourself. I hate you for letting me be taken away by that terrible man that used to rape me in the ass. I hate you for disowning me. I hate you for everything. It should have been the other way around. I should have disowned you!*

Then she fell against the fence, and he lowered her body to the ground while still choking her. He reached up into his pant leg and took out his knife. He slit her throat – the blood spurted out against the fence. John looked down and saw three rings on her finger.

"You weren't married Mom. James was your cousin," he whispered as he pulled the rings off Annie and put them in his pocket. He reached into her pocket and pulled out the contents. He placed the two polished farthings at her feet, Brittania side up. Then he placed the envelope up near her head with the Sussex seal up. He noticed a leather apron lying folded up in the corner of the yard. He had a flash of Eddie telling him they were going to blame the murder on a Jewish man called 'Leather Apron'. Delighted that he wouldn't be caught John carved her up. He pulled up her skirt to expose her belly. Then he slowly cut her stomach open — the way he used to torture the rag heads in Afghanistan. He lifted out her grey, long snake-like intestines and placed them on her shoulder. He thought, *Did you like that, Mom? Did it hurt?*

The fever had him sweating, and he thought he was going to pass out. He quickly cut out her womb. Then he took off his coat and wrapped the organ inside it; he also wiped the blood off his hands. He opened the gate and blended in with the morning crowd going to market.

He got back to Crossingham's and went up to his room where he passed out on the bed. He was delirious and envisioned that his dead mother had snuck into his room and was standing at the door yelling at him with her stomach wide open and her intestines falling out.

She was screaming, "I wish I never gave birth to you John Richard Malthouse. I would still be with Prince Albert if I hadn't got pregnant with you. I wouldn't have had to live in those wretched workhouses. I wouldn't have had to pretend to be married to my cousin. And I wouldn't have been forced to be a whore just to feed myself."

Someone was banging on the door. John managed to get himself up, and he opened the door expecting to see his mother. It was Timothy Donovan, the deputy. He had come up to get the doss money for the night. Timothy asked him if he was alright. John paid him and then laid back down again. First thing in the morning, John caught the train back to York, as his fever had subsided.

Chapter 12

Walter Sickert; Dreams of Crimson Red

During the weekend of September 21st, Eddie and Arthur headed over to see Walter. Eddie told Arthur to play along with him. And Arthur again loved the drama of it all and quickly accepted the opportunity to do some acting. When they reached the studio, Walter was there waiting as arrangements were made. A naked model was there in the studio.

Sickert said, "Eddie, it's been quite a while since I've seen you last. I never got to tell you how much I enjoyed your last painting, the shades of greys and the abstract lines. It still dances around in my head. I've tried to paint something similar myself, but I can't seem to get in the mood."

"I'll tell you what was going on," said Eddie "but she needs to leave first," and he pointed at the model. Walter asked her to get dressed quickly and leave.

After she left, Eddie started his lie, and Arthur played into it perfectly.

"Walter, I need to know who that model was that I painted last time."

Sickert defensively asked, "Why do you need to know?"

"I need to find out who her friends are," demanded Eddie assertively. Then he continued. "She was a friend of Annie; you remember that model that I got pregnant a couple of years ago? Well, she was a friend of hers."

Sickert cleverly asked, "She was a friend of hers, huh? Well, how did they know each other?"

"I don't know how they knew each other, but I remember seeing them together at the party," exclaimed Eddie.

Sickert asked, "What party?"

Arthur quickly said, "A wedding, there was a wedding."

"Whose wedding?" Sickert asked.

Arthur said, "Eddie's, Eddie got married."

"Eddie married who? You're not married," Sickert said as he turned toward Eddie.

"It was a secret wedding," whispered Arthur.

"A secret wedding with whom?" Sickert whispered back.

"It was Annie. I loved her with all my heart. We lived together on the East side for two wonderful years. Until my awful grandmother found out and split us apart," said Eddie almost tearfully.

"That still doesn't explain why you need to know Mary or her friends?" asked Sickert.

Arthur jumped back in, "Eddie had a baby with Annie, right?"

"So," said Sickert.

"Well, one of Annie's friends is probably still taking care of the baby, and we want to find the baby," continued Arthur.

Sickert sarcastically asked, "So why don't you go over to Marylebone and ask Annie Crook where she is?"

"Because she's gone crazy, I'm afraid," said Eddie sadly.

Sickert then said slowly, “Well, she might be crazy, but even crazy people can still tell you who their friends were and who’s watching out for the baby.”

Arthur said, “She’s had surgery, I’m afraid. It’s a new technique developed by our finest surgeon. He takes a hammer and knocks small holes into the head and then they remove a person’s memory.”

Eddie pulled out a pen and demonstrated it on Arthur, “Here, here and here,” as he pretended to be hammering the pen into the temples and then straight forward into Arthur’s forehead.

“They’ve done it a few times now. I’m afraid it still needs perfecting.”

Sickert was still doubtful of their story and decided to accuse Eddie. “Mary was over here right after she saw you, and she didn’t know who Annie Crook was?”

Bertie fired back, “Why were you talking about Annie Crook to her in the first place?” Sickert simmered down.

“It came up in conversation this so-called artist ‘Charles’, that’s what you call yourself, right? I casually mentioned that Charles had gotten a model named Annie Crook pregnant and that she ended up in a workhouse at Marylebone.”

Arthur stepped between Eddie and Sickert who appeared as though they were going to fight.

Arthur said, “Mary, that’s her name, right? Well, she’s just a lying whore. She probably pretended not to know Annie so that you wouldn’t think she did know her.”

Then Arthur turned around almost embarrassed that he had just said that.

Sickert asked, “Well, why wouldn’t Mary want me to know she was a friend of Annie’s?”

“Well, that’s simple,” said Eddie. “She knows that if we find her, we’ll have to kill her.”

“Why would you have to kill her?” asked Sickert intently.

Eddie spewed out, “Because our marriage was in a catholic church. It was saint um, saint um, St Savior’s, yeah that was it. And you’re not allowed by the catholic church to divorce anyone. So legally, we are still married, even though she’s crazy and living in a workhouse. Bless her soul. I loved her so much.”

He paused for a moment and then continued, “But our daughter, Alice, that’s what we named her, is now formally in line for the throne. And Alice is hidden somewhere. And I think Mary was probably the nanny that hid poor Alice.”

Sickert thought for a moment and said, “That doesn’t explain why you would have to kill Mary? That doesn’t make sense!”

Arthur then said, “If a child grows up without the loving care of a parent, and without the education of the best colleges, then the person is not fit for the throne. It will be the downfall of England. The greatest empire in the world.”

Eddie added, “If we can find Mary and her friends, we can find Alice, and I won’t have to kill any more whores.”

Arthur stated, “Eddie and I can raise the child together. She’s probably what only about one or so?”

Arthur had then put his arm around Eddie’s waist.

Then Eddie pushed away Arthur’s arm and said, “But if we can’t find Alice then we need to find all the witnesses of the marriage and kill them all and have the records erased. So, who is Mary and who are her friends or do you personally know where Alice is?”

Sickert didn't know where Alice was, he didn't even know an Alice existed, but he feared they would kill the child. He feared they were lying about raising her right and letting her be in line for the throne.

Sickert said, "My mother and my grandmother were both prostitutes, I hate whores. I don't mind helping you find Mary or her friends, if you're going to kill them. I wouldn't care if you wiped out every whore in London, as long as you let me paint them first!"

Eddie and Arthur looked at each other with shocked expressions.

"So, you'll help us then, Walter?" Eddie asked.

"Yes, I'll help," replied Walter who appeared to be thinking for a moment and then asked, "You don't have anything to do with the murders that have already happened do you?"

Arthur quickly said, "It's Eddie, he's been torturing all of them to find his beloved daughter. It's hard to make those whores talk though. So, he disembowels them first and then he kills them."

Sickert became wildly fascinated.

"Oh, that sounds dreadful, it's awful yet somehow exciting the thought of all that just seems to be giving my Willy a raise." Sickert asked, "Did you find anything out before you killed them?"

"Yes," said Eddie and he went over to Arthur with his pen and pretended it was a knife, he lifted Arthur's shirt and began scribbling on his stomach. Arthur then played as if he were dying and said, "I was Annie's flower girl."

And then he stuck out his tongue and slumped to the floor.

Sickert asked with intrigue, "What about the first one? Oh, what was her name? Where's my newspaper? I've been saving all the articles."

Eddie said slowly and deliberately, "Mary Ann Nichols. You don't need the newspaper."

Arthur jumped in, "She was a bridesmaid."

Sickert then asked, "How come you don't remember the people that attended your wedding?"

Eddie said, "Oh, it was too long ago, and I just couldn't focus on anything except my lovely bride."

Sickert had his back now to Arthur and Arthur started snickering.

"I think you have to flush them out then," he continued thoughtfully, "Wait, wait, wait, a minute," he was staring at the newspaper in his hand which he had quickly fetched. "You have to send a letter to the press or the police or both. Sound as hideous as you possibly can. Let Mary believe you are coming for her if she doesn't tell you who all the friends are that know about Eddie."

"And the baby," Arthur added.

"This is brilliant," said Sickert. Arthur clapped his hands flamboyantly and said, "Let's write a letter right now. You write it Sickert. Our handwriting is too identifiable. Use your artistic ability."

Sickert took out a piece of stationary and brought it over to a roundtable. The three of them then brainstormed. Sickert said, "Let's start with the newspaper. The Central News Agency in London."

Eddie said, "That already sounds too sophisticated, this is going to come back to haunt me, and I'm going to hang for it.

The killer Prince!" Eddie said while making the gesture of being hung by a noose.

"Okay then," said Sickert, "I'll start the letter with 'Dear Boss'."

"This isn't going to work," said Eddie. "That sounds too stupid, and Mary's not going to believe I'm behind the killings. Either way, we are screwed!"

"Not if I get in touch with Mary first and tell her what is going to happen and tell her the letters we are sending to the press are in code so we won't get caught."

Sickert's artistic side was kicking in.

Eddie then had a thought.

"I think the bridesmaid said something about Mary going to the Brittania Public House before she died. Why don't you see if you can find her at the Pub? Don't say too much, try to befriend her, but ask about her friends and if they know about the baby. Don't mention Alice's name."

"I can do that," said Sickert excitedly, "I'm good at acting," he added.

Arthur then said, "I think Eddie and I need to get going on over to Cleveland Street. Why don't you write the letter yourself? We trust you. We'll come back tomorrow morning and see what you've come up with."

Eddie and Arthur were about to leave when Sickert shouted, "Wait, what's your fake name?"

Arthur turned and looked at Eddie and said, "'Jack', call him 'Jack'."

Sickert said, "That's too boring. What kind of knife did you use?"

Eddie thought quickly and said, "The Silversmith for my Hussars made it for the army. We used it to torture people into talking. He calls it 'The Ripper'."

Then Eddie and Arthur left.

Once the door closed behind them, they both burst into uncontrollable laughter. They took turns quoting each other's absurd lies, while they walked over to the boys' brothel. Just before they got there, Arthur stopped Eddie and asked, "Why is he writing a letter to the press again?"

Eddie said, "I don't quite remember. Something about flushing them out."

"That's only going to flush them in," said Arthur.

"Oh, don't worry about it, Arthur. It was just too much fun watching him believing us. I'll try to sort this out in the morning. For now, let's enjoy."

Eddie then knocked on the door. Hammond let them inside. Sickert was writing up the letter, frequently referring back to the newspaper articles he had been saving. He practised all kinds of handwriting styles and various misspelled words to use with different English dialects. After four rough drafts and two long hours, he came up with the final letter. He told himself it was real poetry.

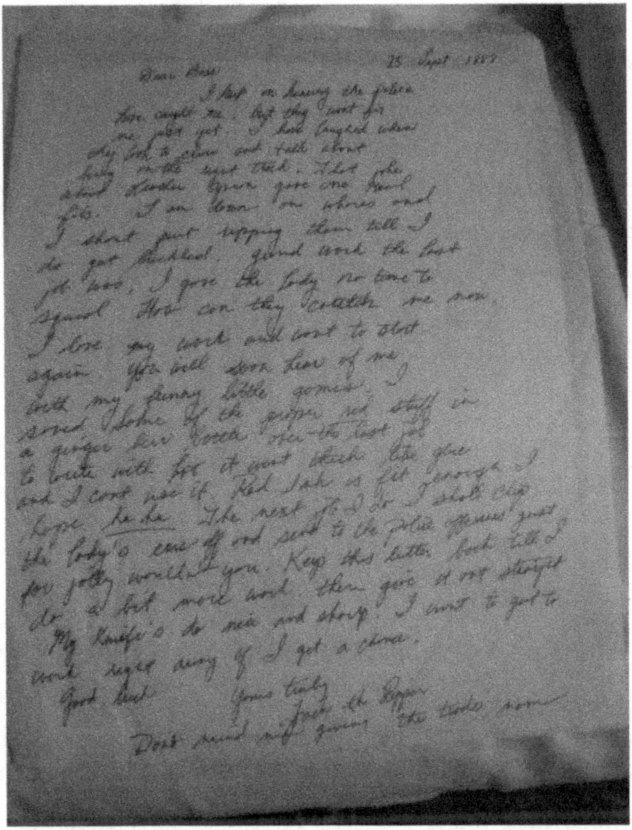

Transcription

Dear Boss,

I keep on hearing the police have caught me, but they won't fix me just yet. I have laughed when they look so smart and talk about being on the right track. That joke about Leather Apron gave me real fits. I am down on whores, and shan't quit ripping them till I do get buckled. Grand work the last job was. I gave the lady no time to squeal. How can they catch me now? I love my work and want to start again. You will hear from me with my funny little games. I saved some of the proper red_stuff in a ginger beer bottle over the last job to write with but it went thick like glue and I can't use it. Red ink is fit enough I hope ha. The next one I do I shall clip the lady's ears off and send to the police officers just for jolly, wouldn't you? Keep this letter back till I do a bit more work, then give it out straight. My knife's so beautiful and sharp. I want to get to work right away if I get a chance.

Good Luck

Yours truly
Jack the Ripper

Don't mind me giving the trade name

Sickert then took off all his clothes and started painting a picture using only red paint. He tried to do it in the abstract way that resembled Eddie's, indeed John's, last painting. He stayed up all night. When Eddie and Arthur returned in the morning, they found Sickert's door was not locked. When they pushed it open, they saw Sickert's motionless body lying naked in the middle of the floor; they thought he was bloody. Arthur gasped and held his scream in, while Eddie ran over to examine the body. When Eddie checked for a carotid pulse, Sickert jolted up.

"What are you doing?" He said to Eddie.

"What are you, doing?" Eddie said to Sickert.

"I guess I fell asleep drinking too much ginger beer," said Sickert.

"Why are you covered with blood?" asked Eddie.

Sickert replied, “Oh, that’s not blood, it’s paint, crimson red, right? Ha. Ha.”

As Sickert got up and began to wipe the paint off himself, he appealed to Eddie, “Look at that piece of garbage,” and he pointed to his painting.

Eddie and Arthur went over and looked at the painting. It was circular swirls of red, only red.

“That’s different,” stated Arthur.

“It’s horrible,” said Sickert. “I can’t do it like Eddie’s masterpiece.”

“Oh, it wasn’t that hard,” replied Eddie sheepishly. “Keep trying. I’m sure you’ll get it. Did you come up with the letter?”

Sickert pointed to the table, “It’s over there.”

Arthur and Eddie picked it up and began to read it while Sickert started telling them, “I’m going over to the Brittania today. I’ll stay there all night if needed. I’ll wait until I see Mary. Don’t worry, I’ll be cautious. I’ll see what I can find out. I’m going to mail the letter right away. Telegraph me tomorrow.”

Sickert then pushed Eddie and Arthur out the door.

Arthur turned to Eddie, “He is so messed up.”

Eddie laughed back.

“I know. That’s why I like him. He’ll probably do a better job of finding Mary and her friends than John did. Maybe he’ll talk that whore into giving him my button back. At least he’s not going to kill them all like my psycho half-uncle.”

“What do you mean?” asked Arthur.

“You didn’t know?” asked Eddie.

“Know what?” asked Arthur.

"The Queen's dead husband, Prince Albert, my grandfather, knocked up my father's nanny and she had John. Didn't you ever wonder why we could almost pass for twins, other than the age?"

Arthur exclaimed, "Good God, where's his mother now?"

"I don't know. They put her in a workhouse and told the staff she was a crazy whore from the east end. That's what we do with all of them. That's what we did with Annie, and that's what should have happened to Mary. Only my crazy fucking uncle keeps thinking about his mother and killing them all."

Arthur asked, "So he believes his mother was a whore from the east end and he's a bastard from one of her tricks?"

"Basically, yeah," laughed Eddie.

Arthur stopped Eddie and said, "Eddie, that's mean, why don't you tell him the truth?"

Eddie said, "It's too complicated now. If he gets caught as the murderer and they discover he's the bastard son of the late Prince Consort, the humiliation the Queen would suffer could ruin our dynasty. Can you imagine the public hanging of the Prince's son?"

Arthur asked, "Well, if you would have told him the truth in the beginning, he probably wouldn't have hated his Mother. He probably wouldn't have snapped on those whores and killed them. Remember he kept saying he killed them because they reminded him of his mother."

"I know," replied Eddie, "my father was only rhetorical when he said he wanted Mary's heart. But everything got so out of control that we're just going to have to take it from here. Probably the best we can hope for is to let him keep killing the whores including Mary. We can then kill him and make it look like a suicide. Then we can allow out enough clues to let the police figure out he was the killer."

"How will we kill him?" asked Arthur.

"Maybe we won't have to. Maybe we can get him to kill himself. That would be less complicated. Keep reminding him that he's a bastard from a whore. Tell him the sins are upon him, and that's why his three sons have died. Tell him his genetics are poison. But don't go overboard with it just yet or he'll do himself off before we get any more out of him. I know, I'll get in touch with the prime minister and let them do some strict religious training. The Freemasons would be good. John's mother was very religious, she was a Quaker, but John rejected the church, probably because of his mother or maybe because of the wars. I don't think he even believes in a God. I'll get that setup, and we'll go from there."

Arthur and Eddie took the train back to York hoping that John would soon be over his fever. When they arrived, however, John was still very ill.

By the time John reached the Barracks in York he was feverish, again he lay down in the bed. He barely talked to his wife. Anne called for the doctor. The military doctor there attended to John. John confided in the doctor and told him he had recently contracted syphilis but that he didn't want his wife to know. The doctor agreed to inform the wife that John had come down with the flu. The doctor suggested to John to send his wife away for a while. John told the doctor to send her hop picking in Kent. Tell her the fresh air would do her some good. So, the doctor went out of the room and spoke with Anne. He told her John had acquired the flu and didn't want her to come in contact with him as he was contagious and it would be dangerous because she was pregnant.

After the doctor left, Anne came into the room. The room smelled awful; it smelled of death she thought. She noticed his coat all balled up in the corner. She went over to straighten it out and hang it up, but John yelled for her to leave it alone. After beginning to pick it up, she looked at her hands and saw blood.

She exclaimed, "John, you must be bleeding."

She started inspecting his shirt and chest, but there were no wounds and no blood.

John said, "Leave me alone, don't come near me, you'll lose another son. Anne, go out to Kent, send for your mother, cousins and your uncle. Have a family reunion."

"But where in Kent?" asked Anne "I don't know the first thing about hop-picking or where to do it?"

John remembered poor sick Dark Annie telling him. "It's in Hunton, near Maidstone."

Then John reached into his pocket and grabbed one of the rings he had taken from Dark Annie and held it out. By now his eyes were closing.

"I love you," he said, and the ring fell to the floor. Anne picked up the ring and put it on; then she gathered up her clothing. Made the necessary arrangements for all of the remaining Hopkins and Howland family members to meet in Hunton near Maidstone. She took the morning train on Monday, September 10th.

Soon after Anne left, Eddie and Arthur showed up. They came into John's room and began kicking the side of the bed to wake him.

"Brilliant work," said Eddie. "I heard all about that whore. It's all over the newspapers. Everyone loves to hear all the gruesome details. The murders give them an excuse now to talk about sex and blood and innards. The photographers can't sell enough of the bloody pictures. What did she know?"

John didn't even open his eyes, but he talked to them anyway.

"Did they find anything around the body?" asked John. Eddie and Arthur turned and faced each other with puzzled expressions.

"What did the police find in the yard?" John asked again.

Eddie referred to an article he was holding in his hand and read, "An envelope with two pills, two farthings, a leather apron, a piece of metal and a broken, empty pillbox."

John then envisioned these in his head as if referring back to a mental photograph of the scene.

Then he told them, "Mary didn't tell her anything. Mary had her read the letter from the Sussex Regiment, London postage."

"Well, did you find out who this Mary was and where she lives?" asked Eddie.

John had a fever and still didn't open his eyes.

"The farthings, what was on the farthings?" John demanded.

"What do you mean?" questioned Eddie.

"Get one, get a farthing out for me."

Arthur reached in his pocket and sifted through his change and found a farthing.

"I've got one here," said Arthur.

Arthur handed it to John.

John opened his eyes for a second and read, "Brittania." "Mary hangs out at the Brittania Public House on Dorset Street," exclaimed John.

"She didn't know anything?" repeated Eddie. "Well then, why did you turn her guts out?"

"She reminded me of my mother again," said John.

Then he remembered and pointed over to the coat wrapped up laying on the floor.

"Over there," said John.

Eddie walked over and picked up the coat and feeling something inside it, he unwrapped the coat and then held up the womb by one of its fallopian tubes.

While exclaiming, "Bloody hell, I thought the stink was coming from you."

Arthur pinched his nose and walked over to have a look-see.

"You've got half her cunnie hanging off of this one."

John said, "Take it to Gull and see if she was pregnant." Eddie wrapped the womb back up in the coat.

John said, "I'm going to need a new coat, and you can have your hat back."

Eddie then wrapped the womb back up in the coat, and he and Arthur left.

Eddie told Arthur, as they were walking down the hall. "Send a message to Sir Charles Warren. Suggest that we are wondering since a leather apron was found near the site if they are going to keep watching him or if they're going to arrest Pizer."

The notice was sent out and Mr Pizer, the Jewish shoemaker, referred to as 'Leather Apron' was arrested. Mr Pizer had been known by many of the locals to grab at the prostitutes and threaten them with his knife saying, "I'm going to cut you up."

That's in turn how he earned his nickname. After four long hours of interrogation, the police let Pizer go. He had a 'rock solid' alibi.

John continued to suffer from the infection. Fevers, night terrors, aching joints and tremors. Eddie and Arthur made visits to John, but he couldn't get up enough strength to even leave his quarters. Eddie decided he would have to do some of the legwork himself. He knew he would be recognised if he spent much time in Whitechapel. So he planned on getting out what little information Walter Sickert, the artist, might know about the model. Sickert dropped off the letter. It was hard for him to contain his anticipation in the hopes that his poem would be taken seriously and printed in newspapers all around the world. He caught a train to Spitalfields and found a nice seat in the Brittania Public House, overlooking the intersection of Dorset and Commercial Street. Sickert had just about drunk himself drunk again on ginger beer when he saw Mary. He ran over to the door and told her he needed to talk to her. He brought her back to the table in the corner.

Then Sickert began to whisper to Mary.

"Mary, what's your last name again then dear for my tax records?"

Mary replied, "It's Mary Kelly, and I'm surprised you even pay tax."

Sickert wrote her name down, and then began to whisper again.

"I came here to ask you if you or any of your friends are interested in doing any more modelling for me?"

Mary made a face and replied, "You want me to model for you, after what happened last time?"

Sickert asked, "What happened last time?"

Mary questioned him, "He didn't tell you what happened?"

"No. Why?" Sickert asked again.

"I don't believe you," stated Mary.

"I think you know."

Sickert whispered, "About the baby and the friends?"

Mary then stood up, "I can't believe it, and he told you everything. That's more than I thought he would have told you."

"Well, he did. I think he's going a little crazy," said Sickert while making a circular gesture with his finger around his ear.

"You better tell me where the baby is Mary," demanded Sickert.

"I don't know what you're talking about," said Mary while trying to pull away. Sickert grabbed her by the hand and sat her back down.

"Fine, play dumb," said Sickert. "You and all your friends are going to wind up painted."

Mary stood up again and grabbed Sickert by the hair.

"I ought to smash your face right now."

Sickert pulled away and said, "Leave me alone, you whore. You're going to get painted red, right? Painted red, right? Ha, ha."

Mary released her grip on his hair as she walked away. Sickert kept repeating, "Remember it, Mary, I'm going to paint you red, right? Ha, ha. Red, right? Ha, ha."

Sickert hadn't realised he had attracted the attention of some people in the pub who by this point were staring at him. He reached into his artist bag and pulled out the red painting from the night before and showed it to the group.

Then he proclaimed proudly, "I'm an artist, and she is one of my models. I told her I wanted to do a portrait of her and she asked if I would do one in red, like this one. I didn't want to, and that's why we argued. But in the end, I agreed. That's why I was saying okay; I'll paint you, red, right? Red, right?"

The crowd didn't seem to care one way or another why he was yelling at her. Threats and violence, bruises and black eyes were a frequent sight in these streets and pubs. Sickert figured he had convinced the crowd he was an honest person, and then pleased with his undercover work, he left.

After he left the pub, he followed Mary. She walked up Commercial Street and turned down Flower and Dean Street. He saw her stop and talk with a woman briefly. Sickert thought Mary was probably telling the woman about how he just threatened her, and she was perhaps one from the wedding Sickert thought. When Mary left, he waited for a minute and then walked over to the woman. He chatted briefly with her; he couldn't take his eyes off her ripped earlobe. He watched his hand reach out and touch it. The lady slapped him, and he left. He could think of nothing else but his poem mentioning clipping her ears. He thought of Van Gogh who clipped off his ear, and he became more and more excited. When he reached his studio near Cleveland Street, he grabbed up a knife and held it to his ear. But he couldn't do it.

He then began painting a picture of the lady's face he saw Mary talking to. He did her face from memory, how could he forget? Then when he finished, he painted over her ears with brown and made red paint dripping out of the holes. He then got excited again and took off his clothes. Then he had this terrible fear.

What if the lady that he arranged to be a model for Eddie last weekend somehow accuses him of being involved with the murders? She saw us all together, he thought. He began to envision the lady without the ears being killed by Eddie very soon, and then the police questioning around and Mary then telling the police that he was threatening her and the people in the pub. *Then the police would come to interview me and what if that model saw them at my house and told them I was conspiring with Eddie? This doesn't make any sense,* he thought for a minute. Then his mind began to race; he couldn't keep up with his thoughts,

What if Eddie conspires against me and is trying to frame me for his murders. Maybe that lady will turn me in for a reward and Eddie and Arthur will hang me out to dry. No, he thought. *What if Mary calls the police right now and tells them she is suspicious of my behaviour. Probably the only woman that would corroborate the story would be that model.*

He continued to think of the various scenarios in his mind. As he mulled over the possibilities, he became more and more confused. Sickert didn't sleep all night long, in the morning he was still worried about the options. He got himself dressed and went over to the model's doss house. He knocked on the door. There wasn't any answer, he asked the deputy where she was and the deputy pointed across the way. Sickert saw the woman haggling with another woman over a loaf of bread. He walked quickly over to her and arranged for her to come back again this Saturday night as 'Charles' was unable to paint her last time. Sickert then reached into his pocket and took out three pounds.

"I'm paying you half now in advance."

The woman was quite happy and announced that she would be at his studio by 3:00 pm on Saturday. Satisfied with this arrangement Sickert headed back into Spitalfields. He brought with him the painting he made of the earless woman in his artist case. He started at the Brittania and then began looking around. He went to Flower and Dean Street and Thrawl Street without success, and then he found her on Dorset Street as she was walking and talking with another man like a married couple. He followed them as they entered a room on Dorset Street. He made a visual memory #38. He stopped a woman and casually asked who lived there.

The lady replied, "A lovely couple: Long Liz and Mike."

Sickert was so happy with his detective work. He got on the train. He noticed he began putting music in his head to the scenes he was observing – different experts from the various music genres, each uniquely perfect to what was going on. The thoughts progressed into Sickert viewing the people and the interaction with each other and the environment as a dance. It now almost didn't seem real to him. *I am in an opera*; he thought:

Life is just one big opera. There is no meaning behind it. It's only for the temporary entertainment of the participants. Maybe we are all just a game. Life is a game. Or life is a play and I am the lead actor and the director. I should head over to the Lyceum Theatre and reserve tickets for Saturday night's 'Doctor Jekyll and Mister Hyde', based on the novel by Robert Lewis Stevenson.

Sickert's thoughts were racing so fast that he couldn't keep his attention on one idea long enough to finish it. On the way home, he sent a coded message to Eddie: that it was imperative to get in touch with him as soon as possible. By the time Sickert got home, he was already writing the next letter in his head.

There would be two women killed this Friday, the model and the woman with the ripped ear, he would hint to this effect, and then the world would know that the letters were real.

He was disappointed when they didn't print his last letter in the news. He began to run home as he couldn't take the anticipation any longer. He opened the door hurried over to the table got his pen and a postcard and his red ink and began to write before he could forget his next masterpiece.

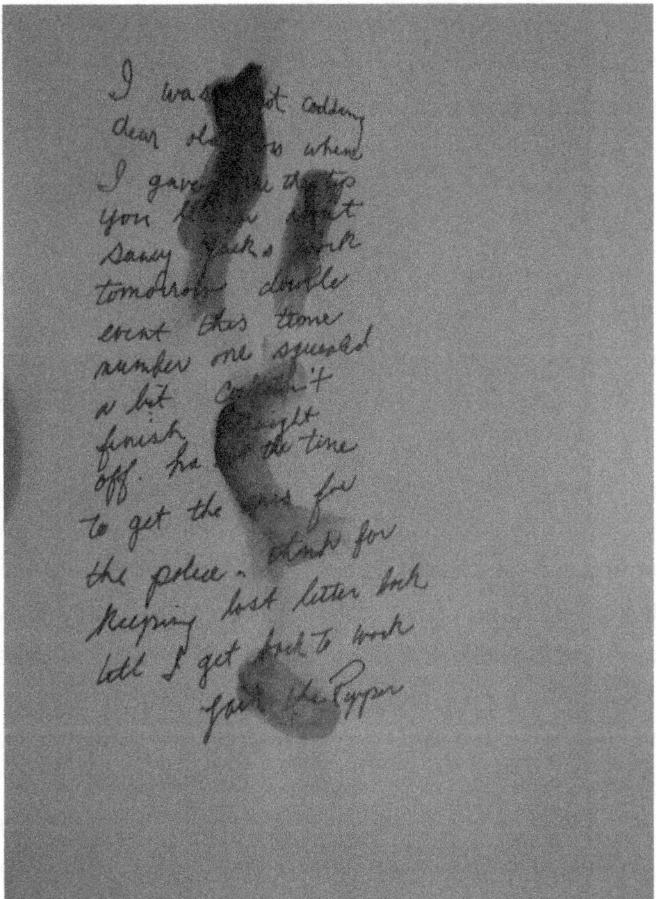
I wa[illegible]t kidding
dear ol[illegible]o when
I gav[illegible] the tip
you [illegible]
Saucy Jack's [illegible]k
tomorrow double
event this time
number one squealed
a bit Co[illegible]'t
finish [illegible]ght
off. ha[illegible] the time
to get the [illegible] for
the police. [illegible]nks for
keeping last letter back
till I get back to work
Yours the Ripper

Transcription

To the Central News Agency.

I was not codding dear old Boss when I gave you a tip, you'll hear about Saucy Jacky's work tomorrow double event this time number one squealed a bit couldn't finish straight off. Had not the time to get ears for police. Thanks for keeping the last letter back till I got to work again.

Jack the Ripper

Sickert knew he had to wait now with the postcard until he heard the word again from Eddie as it was only Wednesday, September 26th.

Back at the Barracks in York, John was finally up on foot. He was walking about and feeling much better. The infection had subsided. Eddie showed up in John's room. Seeing that John was feeling better, Eddie told John that Sickert had been following up on Mary and her friends. What he found out; Mary's last name is Kelly, and he's found two of her friends. Sickert had set up one of them who definitely was a witness, and she would be waiting in his studio at 3:00 pm so that one should be easy; she should be taken out cleanly and quickly. He told John that the other one went by the name of Long Liz and she lived with a man named Mike at #38 Dorset Street. He also mentioned that her earlobe was torn. Eddie informed John to leave by train on Friday and that he would not be accessible for a while as he was going to Abergeldie, Scotland tomorrow and would not return until Sunday, the thirtieth.

He told John if he needed to get more information from Sickert to use Arthur for correspondence. Then he asked about John's wife, and John said she was still out hop-picking.

"I'll send a message that she can come home now," John replied.

Then Eddie said, "Oh, by the way, I have one last thing to tell you. The corporal you were with when you killed Martha Tabram, well he came to me. He knows you've been doing the murders. But it's okay, I trust him, he is one of my best men, and he said he would defend you with his life for what you've done for Country. I've made arrangements with the Bishopsgate Police Station, and he'll be working undercover there, the police have been asking for additional support from the troops since the murders have started. I told them the corporal was my best man and didn't need training. I thought of putting you undercover as well, but they have a strict height requirement of 5'9 or taller. He'll be watching your backside, so you two stay in close touch."

Chapter 13
Fatal Hop Picking

John's wife, Anne had been sent out for hop-picking since September 10th. She had been greeted out there by a cousin-in-law that greeted her at the train station. Her cousin-in-law, Ann Hopkins, welcomed her and her two-year-old daughter Annie, which she nicknamed Pus, at the train station. From there they were brought in a carriage through Coxheath and into Hunton then past the Hunton Church and a little cottage and down a small dirt road into a big farm. Anne thought it was probably 200 acres large, it bordered on a river, and there was a large barn on the property. The farmer said the barn had been built there only some forty-eight years ago or so. A lot of other foreigners were already there. The hop-picking season had officially started over two weeks prior. Almost all of the pickers had taken up lodging in the barn, and so Anne agreed to do so as it could accommodate all of her extended family for the family reunion. Anne's widowed mother, Elizabeth Hopkins (Howland) arrived the next day, and then dribbles of cousins and aunts and uncles from the Hopkins and Howland family came over the next couple of days. Anne was five and a half months pregnant, and her mother was already getting too old for actual picking, so she and her mother and a few other older relatives spent most of the time catching up on the gossip of the family while sitting on the ground on spread out blankets.

This season was one of the worst ever for picking hops. The crops in the surrounding areas were being afflicted by terrible outbreaks of the blight and mould and honeydew. Farmers told the tale of how a plant would look beautiful and green one day and then they would wake up to a black field the next morning. It wasn't worth their money to pay the labourers to pick the limited amounts of crops that hadn't been devastated. Pickers were being turned away. Fights had broken out on paydays as the wages were far below what the workers had anticipated. The word was that Faversham district had a huge fight, a riot with many new black eyes acquired. The event even made it to the newspapers. Thousands of pickers gave up and returned to their homeland – the farm that Anne was staying at though had not been affected. Her cousin that lived there in Maidstone was aware of this blight and is why she picked this particular farm.

After the second week out at the farm, all of the family had caught up enough. They had thoroughly enjoyed the excellent chance of being all together at one time. And everyone in the family left on the weekend of September 22nd, except for Anne, her daughter, Pus and her mother, Elizabeth. Monday, September 24th, Anne began to feel depressed. When asked by her mother what was wrong Anne blamed it on the pregnancy. For the next two days, Anne's depression became worse and worse. Anne didn't want to sit on the blanket out in the sun anymore and instead Elizabeth found Anne crying in the barn in the middle of the day. The last few remaining labourers were outside picking in the crop fields.

Elizabeth asked, “My dear child what is bothering you? I feel now that it is much more than your pregnancy?”

“Oh, Mother,” Anne responded.

“I think I’ve made a mistake by marrying John. I’ve lost three sons of his, but I have a daughter of his that’s well and alive, and he doesn’t even acknowledge her. He acts as though she is invisible. It was her birthday this month and he didn’t even remember. He didn’t even stay home; he went into London on business. Then he returned two days later with a terrible fever. That was the weekend of the awful murder. The doctor there said he had the flu, but he looked much worse to me. At one point, I went to hang up his coat, and he stopped me, but not before I noticed it felt heavy as if something was wrapped up inside of it. When I put it down, I had blood on my hands, but when I checked his body, there were no wounds. And the coat, Mother, the coat smelled like death. Then he gave me this ring. I know the papers have said the victim’s rings were removed from her hand at the time of the murder. Oh, Mother, I fear I have married the devil. I believe he has killed those women. He was away on business in London for the other two murders as well. He’s been acting strangely lately. I know he’s never been very affectionate. I’ve never seen him show much emotion at all. I’ve never seen him cry before, not even after the death of each of his three sons. Maybe I’m misinterpreting things, but I think he’s ‘leather apron’. He always wears a leather apron when he’s shoeing the horses or when he’s working with the silver. Mother, I’m carrying his child. What should I do?”

“Oh, my daughter, I fear for you too, if what you are saying turns out to be true. But under God’s view, you cannot betray your husband. Under God’s ear, you swore to love him no matter what. You must not tell anyone of your fears. Not a word to anyone, do you understand? If John Richard Malthouse hangs for these murders, it will shame the entire family. All your cousins and aunts and uncles that were just here, they all know John Richard Malthouse is your husband, and they all will be disgraced, would you wish that upon your family? I will make the necessary arrangements, and I will come and live with you if you wish. Pus should not grow up with such a father, nor should your unborn child."

Annie quickly replied, "Oh yes Mother, I would love for you to live with me. I have been so lonely these last four years, I have missed you so much. I would never have married John if I hadn't conceived on that dreadful night. Oh, Mother."

The two then both cried and embraced each other.

"Come now, Anne let's walk and get some fresh air, it appears as though Pus has awakened from her nap."

They left the large brick-red barn house with the three large silos and went over to a blanket where Pus had been napping. They picked her up and went off on a short walk. From inside the barn, a lady came out of the shadows. She had had far too much beer the night before and was sleeping off her hangover. She had not intended to be hiding under the covers but was too embarrassed to come out when the conversation started and as the conversation progressed she had listened intently to every word. She wrote down on a piece of paper, John Richard Malthouse. It didn't take the lady long to gather her things up, the drive of the thought of a reward for information as to the killer had all but made her forget her aching head. She didn't want her boyfriend of three years to come with her as she wished to keep all the reward money to herself, even though she considered him as a common-law husband and assumed his last name. John, her boyfriend, saw Mary pass him and go hurrying down the path with all her belongings in hand. He caught up to her, and she made an excuse. They had a small argument but then knowing that it would be too obvious she relented by allowing him to get his belongings and leave also. They didn't have enough money for a train, so they began walking, they caught various carriage rides with other migrant pickers and met up with another couple. All Mary could think about was hurrying back for the reward. The other couple and John did not wish to return to London. The other couple was going on to another hop-picking site in Farleigh, across the Medway's tributaries to Paddockwood. The other lady, Emily Birell, realised that Mary was not going to give in and was going to go on to London with or without them. So, she gave Mary one of her lottery tickets redeemable for a flannel shirt as Mary had used the excuse that she needed to get to London to redeem her lottery ticket also. The two women laughed at the matching lottery tickets; then Mary put them both in her pocket. At the last minute, John decided he would not leave Mary, and he accompanied her on to London.

Mary was still trying to lose John and was unsuccessful until this point. It was now September 28th, Friday evening and it was time to look for a place to sleep. Mary asked John how much money he had and he reached in his pocket and took out a sixpence. Mary took two of the pence and told John to keep the rest. She told him to get a bed at Cooney's, but that she would go to the casual ward in Shoe Lane, Mile End as the deputy there would not turn away people that could not pay. John believed her story, and she was finally rid of him. When she checked into the casual ward on Shoe Lane, she couldn't contain herself, and she blabbed and told Fred the deputy.

"I have come back from hop-picking to earn the reward offered for the apprehension of the Whitechapel murderer. I think I know him." Fred warned her to be careful, and she said, "oh, no fear of that."

The next morning, Saturday, Mary went off for 26 Jewry Street, The City of London Police Department, Scotland Yard as they referred to it. When she arrived, she was nervous as her dress was not up to the standards of the other people going in and out of the office. Scotland Yard was an intimidating place. She gathered up her nerve and headed inside the building. The police officer at the front desk inquired as to her reason for coming, and she said she needed an address looked up. He referred her to the records department. The police officer in front of the records department was also very intimidating, but Mary stood her ground.

"I need you to lookup an address of someone for me," Mary said.

"Who is the person you are inquiring about?" The man asked. Mary quickly responded without having to look at the name she had written down, as she had now memorised it at least a hundred times by practice.

"It is John Richard Malthouse."

"What is the nature of your relationship with this individual?" the constable questioned.

"He is my cousin. He didn't show up at the Malthouse hop-picking family reunion. I wish to know his current address to check and see if he is okay, or if something has become of him."

It was a good lie, and the constable believed her. He said he would have to refer to the last census which was in 1881 and go from there. He prodded for further information.

"About how old is your cousin?" he asked.

"Oh, I am not quite sure, his wife was about ten years younger than my age, so I should say he is about thirty-five to forty years of age."

The constable then said, "Our records are such that it will take quite some time. Would you like to return in a couple of days to give me a chance to look into this?"

"Oh no," Mary quickly retorted. "I wish to wait right here. I'm too worried about my cousin now to even leave," she said.

The constable said, "Suit yourself, but it might take all day."

Mary then saw a bench with an open spot and said while pointing, "I'll just make myself comfortable right over there." Mary then went over and sat down. She waited until just after lunch, then the constable called her over and said:

"I have come up with two men from 1881, census that could be your cousin. I have written them both down for you." And the letter read as follows:

John Richard Malthouse Born abt. 1852 in Winchfield, Essex, England.

Address 23 Firestation, St Botolph Bishopsgate London, England

Folio 72, Page 3

John Richard Malthouse Born about 1851 in Brighton, Sussex, England

Address The Barracks Northgate Canterbury, St Mary, Kent, England

Folio 97, Page 25

Mary put the letter in her pocket and feeling confident that the killer lived in London, she felt sure it was the fireman. Mary began to walk to the Bishopsgate Fire station. It was a long walk by the time Mary reached Houndsditch street. She was almost to the fire station when who should she run into again but John. She quickly thought up another lie and told John she hadn't returned home yet because she decided she was going to try to find her daughter, Annie. She said she would look for her daughter over in Bermondsey. John appeared to believe her story and then Mary said she had to move on. Once around the corner, she waited a minute and watched. John had turned left on Aldgate and was heading back toward where they had considered home for the past six years, Cooney's, on 55 Flower and Dean Street or the common lodging at 32 Flower and Dean Street. She was free of him, at last, she thought then she proceeded to walk right on Aldgate toward the fire station. When she arrived at the fire station, she did a little casual questioning only to find that John Richard Malthouse did work there but that he would be coming on for the night shift. So, Mary being in much need for food and drink, headed over to a pub. She didn't have any money left because she spent it on the last night's lodging, but she cosied up with a man in the pub and got him to buy her a little food and a lot of drink. She began dreaming all the while about the riches she was soon to receive. She had drunk too much and was too excited when she left the pub. She started imitating a fire engine in front of #29 on High Aldgate Street. She was making a spectacle of herself with sound effects of a siren and zig-zagging through traffic until she fell.

A police officer, Constable Lewis Robinson witnessed this and came over and got her. He asked the crowd that was watching her if anyone knew who she was but no one claimed to know her. He pulled her up and leaned her against the shutters, but she fell back over again. So, they took her into custody to the Bishopsgate Police Station to dry out. It was 8:30 pm on the night of Saturday, September 29th.

Previously that day, John and the corporal that was to watch his back took the train to London. They went directly to Sickert's studio on Cleveland Street and then waited and watched from two doors down; they arrived there at 2:30 pm Saturday, September 29th. They saw the model enter Sickert's studio at 2:50 pm. Sickert paid her in the doorway, and then he left. John waited ten minutes for her to undress and then he entered the room. He didn't give her a chance to scream. It was a clean decapitation. Then he cut off her arms and legs. He placed one extremity in each corner of the room. He stood the torso upright in the centre, and he put the head in the garbage can. Sickert had left the painting of the earless woman on the aisle, John took a mental picture of this lady's face and quickly went, locking the door behind him.

Then John and the corporal headed for the East Side. The corporal explained to John that he had to be stationed with the Police at Bishopsgate as it was in the police jurisdiction of the City of London Police, 'Scotland Yard', and Spitalfields and Whitechapel were in the Metropolitan Police Division that was divided up into alphabets, the 'H' division had been responsible for all the previous investigations. But because he was additional manpower and not trained as a bobby, he could not work for the 'H' division Metropolitan Police. He knew John planned to get to Long Liz at 38 Dorset Street, but he encouraged John to make frequent contact with him of his whereabouts. They both agreed to use Commercial Street as their main thoroughfare. The Constable was dressed in a sort of sailorish way; he wore a dark suit with a cutaway coat and a shortly cropped hat with a peak like a sailor's hat, he wore a red scarf around his neck – this was his undercover MO, and he headed over to Bishopsgate Police station to check-in. He arrived there at about 4:00 pm and showed them his paperwork. They told the corporal he was to blend in with the crowd and look for suspicious men or suspicious couples. They gave him a whistle and told him to check in every two hours.

Then he went off to join up with John who was paying Donovan for a night at Crossingham's on Dorset Street. John was wearing a dark suit and the new hat Arthur provided for him. It was a black deer stalker's hat again, and he brought along a long black raincoat as it looked like possible rain for the night. This time, John carried a parcel wrapped in newspaper, it was about six inches in height and eighteen inches in length. He had a full change of clothes in it and a couple of rags. John went over to check out #38 Dorset Street, but there was no sign of Long Liz or Mike. So, John headed up to the old favourite watering hole – The Brittania.

After a bit of casual questioning, John found Mike. After some more casual asking, John found out that Long Liz hadn't stayed with Mike for the past couple of days. Maybe Mary Kelly had warned her about Sickert thought John. So, he set out to find her. He passed the corporal once at 5:30 pm and said he hadn't found Long Liz yet. By 7:30 pm, John was looking for her on Flower and Dean Street from a couple of tips he picked up. He was taken with the preaching in the streets by a well-dressed man. The man was loudly preaching about the evils of the road and the wicked ways of life. He taught of salvation and various other things. John went over to him and asked the man what he was doing. The man stopped his preaching and introduced himself to John as Dr Thomas Barnardo. John told the doctor that he too, was a doctor and that he was looking for a patient who had forgotten her medication. John described the facial features of the woman based on his memory of Sickert's painting. He described her as having excellent characteristics, high cheekbones deep-set eyes, thin eyebrows, a long thin Scandinavian looking nose and light brown wavy hair, and then added that she had a torn earlobe.

Dr Barnardo laughed and replied, "I guess all we doctors notice the fine details of something like that. She's staying right here behind me. She checked in a couple of days ago. A lot of the women are too afraid to walk the streets because of the recent murders. They spend a lot of their time together talking in the kitchen about how nobody cares about them, and how nobody cares if they're murdered. Maybe there is some benefit of the murders after all. It's at least keeping them off the streets. Keep honest men honest. I always say, 'Don't tempt an honest man'."

John had the impression that his last statement had a special meaning. John was, after all, cleaning up the streets for honest Englishmen. If Martha Tabram's solicitation had not tempted him, he never would have contracted syphilis. He would never have murdered her. And he never would have been forced into this never-ending obligation.

John went straight into the doss house there at 32 Flower and Dean Street. The deputy recognised John because he had stayed there before. John said that he's just taking a beer in the kitchen. He headed over to the kitchen and just as the preacher had described there were many women gathered in the kitchen. He instantly picked out Long Liz. He got a beer and sat behind them within close range. He listened to everything they were talking about but at least if this Long Liz did know anything she wasn't talking about knowledge of the murderer or of Mary Kelly. At about 8:00 pm, the women regretfully decided they had to go out and make enough money for tomorrow's food, drink and bed. So, the women got up their nerve and headed out into the streets. John immediately got up and then followed Long Liz from a safe distance. At the door to the lodging house, he saw Long Liz give a piece of green velvet to another lady and asked her to keep it safe until the morning. John followed Long Liz around. He could see that she was a seasoned prostitute. She appeared to be able to enter a pub and quickly size up the prospects of her solicitation, and if there weren't much of a chance, Long Liz would be in and out of a pub within a minute. At 10:30 pm, John had been waiting outside the Bricklayer's Arms Public House on Settles Street, North of Commercial Street for over half an hour. Figuring that long Liz was being successful, John felt safe enough to venture away back to commercial and catch up with his corporal. At 10:30 they found each other on Commercial Street. John updated the corporal about finding Long Liz and suggested the corporal set the woman up so that she would feel safe with John. John told the corporal that Long Liz appeared to be hanging around Berner Street and suggested they walk back to the pub in which she was last seen. As they walked back to Berner Street, they talked. John asked the corporal for an update. The corporal said that one of the Bobbies had picked up a woman too drunk to provide her name. The corporal was laughing.

He said, "They told me, when they asked what her name was, she said, 'Nothing my name is nothing'."

John asked why she was picked up, but the corporal didn't know. John and the corporal were walking back towards the pub when they saw her standing in the doorway with a man. John and the corporal quickly split up. Long Liz and the man were kissing and hugging as they stood in the doorway. It was raining somewhat, and they didn't want to go out. The man was short with a dark moustache. He was wearing a billycock hat and a mourning suit. The man was very Jewish looking. Two other men that looked like labourers approached the entrance, but the man and Long Liz wouldn't move out of the way. They just kept kissing and hugging. One of the labourers said to the man:

"Would you like to come back inside maybe and have a drink with us?"

The man, however, did not answer he did, however, step aside. As the two labourers passed by the couple into the pub, one of the labourers called to Long Liz, "That's leather Apron getting around you."

John then watched as the corporal quickly caught up with the couple. He had some words with the man, mostly concerning his Jewish heritage and how Long Liz would be much better off with an English man like himself. The corporal drove the man away with his harassing and then he began chatting up Long Liz. He found out that other than her boyfriend everyone knows her as Long Liz. She then started on the 'poor me' spiel that she frequently used to get sympathy.

In 1878, Princess Alice, a saloon steamship that she and her entire family were on, collided with the steamer, Bywell Castle, in the Thames. Her entire family to include her husband and all her children, along with about 600-700 other people all drowned. But she had managed to climb up the mast of the sinking ship when the man above her kicked her accidentally in the mouth. She turned and showed him. She showed him how she lost all her teeth on that bottom side. She then claimed that it cracked the roof of her mouth and then finally his shoe had caught her earing and it ripped her ear right through. Liz claimed that the only remaining relative left in London is a nephew that works for the police department. The corporal asked her what her nephew's name was and she said, Frederick Stride. Then the corporal asked what division and she said the Metropolitan Police. The corporal then pulled Liz into a doorway on Berner Street and began to kiss her and fondle her. She, however, did not resist him. The corporal turned her back toward the street and motioned for John to start approaching. Then the corporal started asking Liz about the price. They discussed what the services were.

The corporal agreed to an upright and then told her, "When we do it, you can say anything but your prayers because I guarantee you're going to be squealing when you feel the size of it, why my woody's probably the biggest cock in London. I should only pay you half price for letting you ride it."

Then John interrupted the corporal.

"Is this man harassing you, Madame? I couldn't help but notice from across the street that he seemed of a bad character. I saw you earlier this evening in the kitchen of the lodging house. I am staying there myself. Would you care to leave this man and join me for a walk? I passed a man selling grapes. Would you like me to buy you some grapes?"

Liz played right into their hands, and she walked off with John. The corporal then headed back to the station to check-in.

John was a master at portraying different personas. He enjoyed the challenge of fooling people. It was a form of a power play for John. He knew he was going to kill this lady, but he wanted to milk out everything about her. He tried to strip her of her protective shell, and expose her naked insecure soul, then kill her. He had all night long, and he wanted to take his time. He did buy her the grapes, and then they talked. John found that she was originally from Sweden. Then he heard all about her boat colliding, and family dying, ripping ear, losing teeth, breaking the roof of the mouth story. Then he peeled off her outer shell. He got her to confess that she wasn't happy at all with the life that she was leading. She told him how she tried at first to make an honest living as she was both a seamstress and could crochet. She told John how little by little the Jews had taken over the business and dominated the market, petticoat lane. They had the machines where they could mass produce. They worked their employees long and hard, and they worked long and hard too. All the women that were seamstresses are now prostitutes because of the Jews, she said. She further went on to tell John that she was not religious and therefore had no prejudice against them for their lack of belief in Jesus. It was just because of how they treated people, how they viewed themselves to be better than others.

Liz said, "You'll never see a Jewess prostitute."

She resented them, and added, "The irony of it is that I even have to clean up after them. I made six shillings today cleaning up their fucking beds."

Then she continued to tell him how she had taken up with a man named Michael Kidney for the past three years. They lived together on Dorset Street, but that they had had a fight and she left him two days ago to go and stay on Flower and Dean.

"On the meanest street in London."

She then bragged: "I've been arrested eight times in the past twenty months for being drunk and cursing at the Queen's Head Pub."

Then John stopped her from walking, and they stood together in an entrance to a yard just outside of a club. John now leaned against the wall and took out his pipe and was just about to light it when the corporal came walking up quickly.

"John come on quickly."

The lady then noticed that the two men knew each other, figured out that she had been set up.

She tried to run away, but the corporal grabbed her by the right hand. As she resisted, she fell with him onto the street and let out three screams. A Jewish-looking man across the street saw this and moved to get a better view of the situation.

The corporal then yelled: "What are you looking at Lipski?"

The man became embarrassed and started to walk away. John had kept his composure during all of this. He lit his pipe (anyway); then propped his right foot up against the wall.

John pulled his knife out from under his pant leg. The corporal had now pulled the lady up to her knees. He was behind her also on his knees and had his left arm wrapped across her chest. He was holding her tightly under her right arm. With his right arm, he covered her mouth and tipped her head back to expose her neck. John was the best swordsman in the troop, and his corporal knew it. He knew he wouldn't get nicked. John then walked past and slid his knife gracefully through her throat at his waist level and then proceeded to follow the Jewish man quickly and scare him away. It worked. The Jewish man was frightened off. John quickly returned to the corporal who had now lowered Liz to the ground. She had dropped the grapes she had been holding.

John reached into her pocket and quickly checked the contents. Then he took one of the bags of cashews and placed it in her hand. Then he picked up the grapes. The corporal told him to follow him quickly, and then he told John the details as they hurried together.

"After I left you last, I went back to the station. The drunk woman I told you about earlier woke up. When they asked her what her name was, she said, 'Mary Ann Kelly'.

"I know we're still looking for the pregnant Mary Kelly that has the Prince's button. So, I went over to her without the other Bobbies noticing anything much, and I chatted her up a bit. She told me she was going to get the reward later the next day. She wouldn't let me know the name of the individual but told me he was a fireman. When I asked her to at least tell me his first name she said:

"'I'll tell you his initials, they're 'J.R.M'.'

"I thought that too much of a coincidence, so I ran right over here to get you. I think they're getting ready to release her."

John and the corporal now began to run down Commercial Street toward the police station. When they noticed they were about to run right past a police officer, they stopped briefly for a minute, and John told the bobby.

"There's been another murder, down there on Berner Street, it's another woman."

When the constable left, they continued to run again. As they approached the police station, the police were releasing Mary. The corporal handed John his red scarf and motioned to John that the lady walking away was the one and he then entered the station. The corporal told them he was checking in again and made no mention what so ever about the murders. He said he was going to sit for a few minutes and take a load off his feet. It wouldn't be long before the head police station would be contacted. He thought this would shift all the police attention off of him. He figured much of the police force would now be drawn to the other side of Whitechapel.

John started moving in for the kill. He could feel his pulse now pounding in his right temple. He could feel his animal side, his atavistic instincts coming in to control his mind. Was this the real Mary Kelly and how did she know his initials? Now it was personal. John pulled in the reins on his anger before she would feel his eyes piercing through the back of her head. He quickly caught up with her as she headed down Houndsditch toward Aldgate, then she made a quick turn onto Duke Street. While John was following her, a man recognised him when he passed the Imperial Club.

He yelled, "Hey, Buck's Row," to John.

John turned toward the man. He was the butcher from #1 Hutchinson Street. It had been over twenty years, but the man remembered John as the teenager who brought horse meat into the market. John knew his name was Mr Levy and John had always liked him. But now this man was going to interfere with John's kill, and like a lion that is threatened by another lion, John would have to show who was stronger. Just as he communicated with the horses, John stared intently at the man while thinking *BEWARE.* The man turned back around, and he went back toward the entrance. Then John had to walk quickly to catch up with Mary. He shouted to her once she was in the church passage.

"Are you the famous Mary Kelly?"

Mary turned around to him puzzled and said: "What's that all about?"

John replied, "Oh, one of my friends back there is a police officer. I'm a police officer myself, but I'm undercover now. There's not too many of us undercover, but we're doing it to try to catch the murderer. Anyway, after you were let out of there one of them suggested I follow you home to make sure you make it home safely. I heard you had had quite a bit to drink. So, I've been following you, but I figured maybe I should introduce myself and escort you to your home. That would probably be even better."

Mary was very flattered by the thought that anyone cared that much about her.

"Well, I'm flattered," she said.

"May I ask where you live?" John questioned.

"Oh, I've been staying with my old man at 55 Dorset Street," replied Mary.

"But that's the other direction," observed John.

"Well, I just need to make a little stop first," said Mary.

"And should I dare ask where that little stop might be?" asked John

"I'm just going to go over to the fire station and inquire about my cousin," said Mary.

"You have a cousin that's a fireman?" asked John.

At that moment, John saw Mr Levy again. Mr Levy was scared enough by John earlier to seek the escort of two other Jewish men. John was facing them, and Mary had her back to them. John could feel his mind sending out a silent message to the men *BEWARE*, and John felt as though his eyes were communicating with Mr Levy, such as in the way he communicated silently with the horses. As the men passed, John said, "I'm sorry what were you saying?"

"That I'm going to visit my cousin," repeated Mary.

"Oh, that's right. I have a lot of friends at the fire station. We policemen and firemen always get along well together. Maybe I know your cousin. What's his name?"

"It's John Richard Malthouse," replied Mary.

"John Richard Malthouse. Is that what you said?"

"Yes," replied Mary, "he's my cousin."

"Oh, that's wonderful," said John. "You see I know him too. He's an excellent friend of mine. So, let's go walk to see him together?"

Then Mary and John began to walk toward the fire station together. John questioned Mary.

"So tell me, Mary, what pressing business is it that you have with your cousin, John Richard Malthouse, that can't wait until tomorrow. It's already past one in the morning." Mary now knew that John was going to catch her in a lie when they showed up together in the fire station. The John Richard Malthouse fireman there would acknowledge that he didn't know Mary. So, Mary stopped inside Mitre Square. She turned to John and said, "I can't go on with this any further. Your friend John Richard Malthouse is not my cousin. He's an evil man."

"How bad of a man is he?" whispered John.

"I think he's the murderer," whispered Mary.

"I think you might be right," whispered John. "You know I've always thought he was a little messed up in the head you know? Is that what you think about him too?" whispered John.

"Oh, I've never actually met him," whispered Mary.

"You haven't met him? Then why do you think he's the murderer?" whispered John.

"Well, it wasn't me that thought it. It was his wife," replied Mary.

"So, you know his wife, Anne, then do you?" asked John.

"No not exactly," replied Mary.

"Well, how is it exactly that you came into the knowledge that John Richard Malthouse is the murderer from his wife when you don't even exactly know her?" whispered John.

Mary said, "When I was hop-picking in Kent, I saw his wife telling her mother that she believed her husband was committing the murders."

"Oh, I see," said John. "You saw her. But that doesn't explain how you came into finding that he's a fireman."

"Look here," said Mary as she pulled out the paper from her pocket that she got at the Records Department from Scotland Yard. She handed it over to John.

"I went to the police this morning. I had to wait all day practically, but they looked it up for me and wrote down the information."

John looked at the letter and said: "But this lists two different John Richard Malthouses?"

Mary whispered back, "Since the other one is all the way over in Canterbury and because he's a soldier, I figured this one must be the right one."

"Oh, you are a brilliant lady. Hold this for a second," John said while he handed the paper back to Mary. He bent down and reached under his pant leg.

"Now I have something to show you too," John whispered.

"What is it?" asked Mary. John then stood up and showed her his knife.

"Why are you showing me your knife?" asked Mary nervously.

John then leaned right up to her ear and whispered: "Because I'm the other John Richard Malthouse."

Just as Mary's panic reached the expression on her face, John leaned back and slashed at her throat before she could scream, he cut right through her vocal cords. He stood smugly standing over her as he watched her drop to the floor.

"Did you really think you were going to have them hang me from a noose?"

John then took the letter out of Mary's weltering grip. And he set it out on the ground where he could see it. Then John carved out his last initial across her face 'M'. Then he took his knife and began picking away at her eyes, making little incisions.

He whispered "You shouldn't have been so nosey, you're not supposed to spy on other people, it's not nice. You should have kept your eyes, and ears," with that he cut through her right ear, and it fell off onto her shoulder, "out of other peoples' business."

Then John backed up and watched as Mary attempted to move but couldn't. She was breathing very softly now that there wasn't much life left in her. Mary was now lying flat on her back. John then pulled up her three layers of skirts. She wasn't wearing any undergarments.

John said: "That's disgusting; you must be a whore as well as a snitch."

John then pulled up Mary's right leg as he kneeled between her legs. He put the point of his knife slowly into her just under the breastbone and then he pulled down through her abdomen all the way to her pubic bone. He cut into a portion of her intestines and then scooped them outward with his knife. He had punctured the large bowel, and faecal matter was oozing out into the abdominal cavity. "Now let me see if I remember which shoulder you're supposed to throw the bowels over with a traitor. I think it's the right."

And then John pierced the end of the bowel and brought it over the shoulder and then hesitated and brought it over to the ground. Then he severed off a two-foot portion.

"I'll tuck this little piece under your left arm to make sure everyone knows I throw your guts over your right shoulder on purpose."

John then tucked the cut portion under her left side and the rest he placed back over the right shoulder. Then John cut out her womb. He had an odd thought, and he felt compelled for some reason to take out a kidney. With one quick swipe, he took out her left kidney. Then knowing he didn't have much time left as he and Mary were standing in the shadows of the corner the first time he saw a constable with a light walk past. That was already about ten minutes ago. He quickly lowered her skirt and cut off a portion of her apron he wrapped up the womb, the kidney and the letter in this piece of cloth and then he left her mangled remains.

Chapter 14

Lies Coding and the Freemasons

John realised he could not return to the Crossingham's; there would be far too great of a chance of capture. He headed north towards the city. He had walked a few hundred yards and then opened his package he quickly changed his pants as they were splattered with blood, then he put the contents of the piece of the apron as well as his blood soiled pants into his package. He wiped off his hands on the apron piece and then dropped it on the ground. He took a few deep breaths and then tried to calm down. During the entire killing, his adrenaline had been coursing through his arteries. His senses heightened to the point where he could hear a mouse coming and notice the flickering of light from a half a street block away. He felt like an animal, like a predatory animal – one of the best animals. He was the king of animals, the animal-human – the top of the food chain. He took a few deep breaths and then looked around. He was on Ghouston Street in the stairwell of an entrance to some residences of a building called the Wentworth Buildings. All about him was Jewish tenement housing and behind that the dominated Jewish market. He remembered that Levy recognised him and like any other predator that wants to leave a warning to 'Beware' he very purposefully reached into his pocket and took out a piece of chalk and wrote on the wall above the bloody part of the apron.

"The Jewes are the men that will not be blamed for nothing."

John then made his way down to the end of Ghouston Street where the abandoned old Aldgate East Station remained. He descended inside and found a quiet, dark spot where he could safely sleep. He wasn't able to sleep, but at least he rested there securely.

In the light of the morning, he decided to go to the heart of the giant, to the centre of the cause of his situation, the heart of his motherland, the land that he vowed to protect with his life, the home that he fought for and the nation that he killed more men for than he could count. This was the place he was going to hell for, England. London was the heart of England, and he would make a bullseye in the exact centre of London, Kentish Town. John took the underground to Kentish Town and then he went into a pub there called the Nelson Tavern on Victoria Road. He had a couple of pints to calm down; then he went out to relieve himself in the outhouse building. As he sat there on the crapper, he opened up the parcel and took out the kidney. He tried to fit the organ into his beer bottle but it wouldn't fit, so he cut it in half. John put half of the kidney in the beer bottle. John took out and opened up the womb with his knife and checked it for a foetus. There was no foetus; this was not the pregnant Mary Kelly. John removed the letter from 24 Jewry Street, City of London Police Records Department: With the listings of the two John Richard Malthouses. He took out a pen and crossed out the Fireman and circled the soldier, then put everything back in the parcel:

the womb, the other half of the kidney, the bloody pants and the letter. He finished and left the package right there in the outhouse in the dead centre of London. He couldn't have left a better clue than that of what he thought of England.

Then he headed for Cleveland Street to dispose of the body left at Sickert's. At 9:00 am on that morning of September 30th, the owner of the Nelson Tavern went out to use the outhouse. The door was hinged so that it pushes in, so when he opened the door, it pushed the package against the wall. The owner looked at the package but didn't think anything of it. Then at 10:00 am, an hour later, a man named Mr Chin went out to use the outhouse, as he sat there he saw the package too, only he recognised it to be like the one the police were describing the murderer was carrying the night before.

'About six inches tall and eighteen inches in length wrapped in newspaper.'

Mr Chin quickly reported it to the Kentish Town police station. Then at 10:15 am another man went into the outhouse when he saw the package he set it outside the door so that the owner could retrieve it without disturbing him. A stray dog picked up the scent of blood and quickly located the package, the dog grabbed up the package and brought it out to the street, and then ripped it apart and immediately ate the womb and kidney. The letter from the records department blew down the street. By the time a constable arrived to retrieve the package, he had arrived only to find a pauper in the process of picking up the bloody pants for his own use. The constable quickly entered the pub to inquire about the whereabouts of the package. The owner told him that he had seen a package in the outhouse an hour and a half or so ago but did not think anything of it at the time.

The constable asked: "Didn't you tell a Mr Chin to bring you that package from the outhouse?"

"No," replied the owner.

The constable figured maybe Mr Chin didn't want to move the package to disturb any potential evidence. So, they both headed out to the outhouse together only to find that the package was gone. The constable immediately realised that that was what he must have seen in the street. He ran back around to the street but by this time, the pauper had left with the bloody pants, and the ripped up remains of the package had been run over more than a couple of times. The constable picked up the remnants and brought them back to the station. Upon study, all that they could find were blood stains and a few pubic hairs.

When John arrived at Sickert's studio on Cleveland Street, it was just in time to see Eddie and Arthur entering the studio. John quickly went over, and because the door wasn't locked, he entered the studio, locked the door and turned around. The scene that was laid out before him was like nothing he had ever imagined. His attention was drawn first to a naked torso of a body lying on the middle of the bed. He was then attracted to the head of the lady that was sitting on a crystal cake platter in the centre of the round table. The arms and legs were bundled together and lay in the firewood tray beside the fireplace. Sickert was standing naked and covered with red paint. Arthur was vomiting on the floor in the corner of the room, and Eddie was sitting on a chair bent over to allow the blood to rush to his head so he wouldn't faint. Then John noticed a series of three painted canvasses propped against the wall to dry. The colours on the canvas were dark muted shades of grey. The paintings were in an impressionistic style; they were the most hauntingly beautiful still lifes John had ever seen. The torso of a beautifully proportioned woman lying on the bed. The head of a beautiful woman on a crystal cake plate, with a bloody knife resting beside the cake which sat on the table beside some wilted flowers and a glass of wine. A fireplace with the embers of a dying fire and the arms and legs bundled beside it. John began to laugh, he didn't know what else to do. And then Sickert started to laugh. Eddie sat up in the chair, and he began to laugh, and finally, Arthur wiped the vomit from his mouth and he began to laugh. And they laughed, and they laughed and they laughed.

When they had finally laughed themselves out, Sickert still naked, took a seat on the bed beside the torso. John sat down at the table beside the lady's head. Eddie stayed put in the chair that wasn't near any of the body parts. Arthur sat down on a stool behind the aisle that was in the corner of the room where he had vomited. Sickert broke the silence first.

"Eddie, why did you leave this headless woman in my studio in the first place?"

John said, "He didn't leave the body there, I did!"

Sickert quickly turned to Eddie and asked: "Who is he, I thought you said you were killing the women."

Eddie replied, "Not exactly, you see he's Dr Gull and killing the women for me. Because he has a much better knowledge of anatomy and my hands are too shaky from syphilis to be able to do those things myself," Eddie lied.

Sickert then turned and looked at John and stated: "He's not Dr Gull, Dr Gull is old, and he's had a stroke!"

Arthur quickly said, "Oh no, he's not Dr Gull, he's the carriage driver for Dr Gull. He drives the carriage of Dr Gull around and then after Dr Gull is through butchering the women in the carriage he deposits the women's bodies and lays them out according to Dr Gull's directions. The carriage driver over there is pretty dumb, so you probably won't get much information from him."

John then pretended to look pretty dumb and replied, "That's right, I do as the doctor says. I always do what he tells me, right?"

Eddie then turned to John and said: "Yes, you've been a good servant."

Sickert looked pretty confused and then asked: "Why is the doctor doing the murders for you?"

Arthur said, "It's because the doctor loves Eddie."

Sickert then made a strange face and turned to Eddie and asked: "You and the doctor are in LOVE?"

Eddie made a glower at Arthur and then turned to Sickert and said, "Oh, it's not that kind of love. He loves me like a father. He views me as his son. He's just so mad that some whore gave me this horrible case of syphilis that he wants to wipe out the entire population of whores."

Sickert looked confused and asked, "Isn't he afraid of getting caught?"

Then John, catching on to what Eddie and Arthur were doing, responded while trying to put on his best dumb accent and facial expression, "Yes, the doctor is afraid of getting caught. On this last one, he killed last night he had me lay out the lady's intestines over her right shoulder and then had me scribble a message on the wall that he thought Sir Charles Warren would be able to figure out."

Eddie then turned to John and asked, "Has the good doctor mentioned to you why he thought Sir Charles Warren would understand this message?"

John then replied, "Something to do with him becoming the next master mason and something else about a traitor."

Sickert looked very confused and asked, "What the devil is going on?"

Eddie then responded to Sickert, "Sir Charles Warren is a member of the Freemasons society. It is a society comprised mostly of the upper crust of civilization, formed to try to influence political decision making. Although started by horse whisperers in Scotland, it has spread rapidly through our country as we are the world's empire. Originally, when one was allowed to be indoctrinated into the society, they had to proclaim no belief in a supreme being. They had to proclaim that they understood each person is their own God. That people are Gods and that each person, therefore, has control over their destiny. That a person could choose to live a peaceful, helpful, moral life and then enjoy the riches of the emotions that come from living that way, thus creating their own heaven: right here, right now, on earth. However, people that live a wicked, immoral life of a criminal nature will thus accrue negative self-hate emotions that go along with that, thus creating their own hell. But recently it seems that the Catholic church has poisoned or infiltrated through the Masonic society by way of the Pope's recent appointment of Archbishops and Cardinals into England's political arena. This heavy influence now of religion in the Freemasonry society has made the progress turn-about face. Now to join the brotherhood, you must swear your allegiance and belief in only one supreme God. There now is a lot of talk about rebuilding King Solomon's temple. There is also a lot of talk about the traitors and how they were slaughtered. It's now essentially a front for white Christian supremacists. Anyway, help me out on this one, Arthur; I forgot where I was going with it?"

Arthur then roused up and added; "Basically, what Eddie is saying is that Sir Charles Warren head of the Police Department is also going to become the next Master Mason of the Coronati Lodge. He thus has a very vested interest that the image of royalty and England's world supremacy not be smeared with a scandal like a murderous grandson of the Queen who is in line for the throne. So, if he can identify enough coded messages by the murderer to indicate that the murderer is a Freemason and that the murders have something to do with royalty then hopefully he will make the evidence vanish. That's why the doctor and his driver over there shouldn't be afraid of being caught."

Sickert had been listening to the whole conversation very intently and then concluded, "Wow, that's heavy. So where do we go from here?"

John then began to talk.

"Well, the doctor still is a little afraid of being caught, and he wants me to deposit of this body in a way that's very threatening to a possible traitor such as the City of London Police Department on 24 Jewry Road, Scotland Yard." Eddie turned to John and said, "Do you think the doctor would approve dumping the body at the proposed site for the New Scotland Yard? The current Scotland Yard is too heavily guarded ever since the Fenian attacks; it would be too risky to dump the body there."

John then replied, "I think the doctor would very much enjoy that. Would you see if you could borrow the doctor's carriage for me so I can dump the body off tonight?"

Sickert quickly raised his hand and began pleading, "Can I keep the head a little longer? I have another painting I want to make as the skin begins to rot away. I'll get rid of the head later. I promise."

Eddie replied, "I'll get a carriage for you tonight. And Sickert you can keep the head a little longer if you deliver another message for me to Mary. Write this down, so you tell her these exact words."

Sickert then got out a piece of paper.

"Tell her, 'The necessary investigations have been completed. At this point, we want to take the baby, and we will leave you unharmed. We will give you 500 pounds for the exchange. We will get back in touch with you once you have had time to think about it'."

Sickert begged, "Can I mention the red, right, ha, ha to her?"

"No," said Eddie. "Keep it as I just told you."

Sickert looked very disappointed and asked, "Well then, can I write some more letters? I'm sure they are going to publish the one about the double event. Isn't it funny how that turned out? You killed the third one but never put this one out on the street. So that still made just two. That is such a coincidence that is just so funny. I think maybe I'm clairvoyant or something and I just knew not to dump this one myself."

Sickert then looked very disappointed and asked John, "Did the doctor cut off any ears, do you know?"

John replied, "Yeah half an ear from the last one."

Sickert excitedly asked, "Do you have the ear by any chance?"

John replied, "No."

Sickert then hopefully asked, "Do you have any body parts at all?"

John then had a sudden recollection and took out the beer bottle from inside his coat and proclaimed, "I've got half a kidney in here."

Sickert was thrilled and immediately got off the bed and took the beer bottle from him and brought it back to his bed caressing the bottle as if it were a crown jewel.

Eddie and Arthur began to laugh. Arthur asked, "Why on earth did you take her kidney? I thought you were in the habit of taking her womb?"

John quickly said while closing his eyes and trying to remember, "Give me a minute…I remember now. The second one's name was Mary Kelly, that's why I killed her. I checked the womb myself, and it didn't have anything inside it. I remember I didn't have a chance to take the kidney from the first one as I was in a real hurry."

Eddie asked, "Why did you want the first one's kidney?"

John then closed his eyes again for a moment and said, "Her common-law husband's last name is Kidney. I never got to find out if she knew anything, but maybe the husband does. I'll have to question Kidney."

Sickert looked up from his stare at the beer bottle and asked, "Which kidney is it?"

"The left," replied John.

Sickert then replied, "That driver sounds almost as smart as the doctor?"

John then replied, "Well, guess what? If you do write a letter on his behalf will you make the return address 'From Hell' because that's where he said he and I are living. We're living in the hell that we made for ourselves just like the old Free Masons used to teach."

Sickert thoughtfully asked, "Is the doctor not religious?"

John replied, "Oh, he's very religious, he just doesn't want to believe that there could be such a thing as a supreme God that had enough magical power to create us, but that does not possess the power or does not possess the desire to even save us from ourselves. As the doctor said, 'No God would be mean enough to do that; we do it to ourselves'."

Eddie and Arthur left to make the arrangements for a carriage for John. Eddie would go back to York and Arthur would bring the wagon to John later that night. John laid down on the floor and said he would try to sleep as he hadn't slept for quite a while. Sickert then still naked got out a piece of stationery. He decided to send the letter to the head of the newly formed Whitechapel Vigilantly group.

The group formed back on September 16th. The group offered one of the highest rewards which consisted of hundreds of volunteers that would take shifts to help patrol the area. Sickert wrote:

From Hell,
Mr Lusk,
Sor

I send you half the Kinde I took from one woman prasarved it for you tother piece I fried and ate it was very nise. I may send you the bloody knif that took it out if you only wate a whil longer.

Signed
Catch me when you can Mishter Lusk.

Then Sickert smashed open the beer bottle to get at the piece of the kidney, and he put it in the wine glass on the table that was sitting beside the head. He needed to save it until he had his meeting with Mary Kelly.

Arthur showed up with the carriage when it was dark. Arthur was both the driver, as he was in charge of being the head of the stables, he was quite adept at driving a six horse-drawn carriage. The horses were all beautiful shiny and black, perfectly paired with each other. Their breath was steamy in the crisp air; the wagon was a closed type just as black and shiny as the horses. John wrapped up the body parts in Sickert's linen and loaded them into the carriage.

Sickert sadly said, "I'm going to miss that torso. She was a beautiful Greek sculpture, don't you agree?"

John replied, "Yeah, it's a ripe piece of art that you did to that one. Maybe I should take some lessons from you." Then John climbed inside the carriage and Arthur made the horses trot off. Once they reached the site of the planned New Scotland Yard, John quickly took out the wrapped-up torso and carried it down into the cellar. Then he unwrapped it and stood it up on the floor like a statue. He jumped back inside the carriage while instructing Arthur to drive to the bridge. Arthur made the horses trot off again. Once the carriage was on the bridge, John opened the door and quickly threw out the bundle of legs and arms and watched them splash into the Thames.

Now it was time to do the thing that John was most dreading. To return home to the pregnant wife who suspected he was the killer. Arthur dropped John off close to the train station. When John returned to York, he was surprised to see that his mother-In-Law, Elizabeth Hopkins had moved in with them. His wife told John she had encouraged her mother to take care of Pus, to become the nanny so to speak. Anne suggested that this would relieve her from many of the duties that might negatively affect the pregnancy. So, Elizabeth and Pus shared one bedroom, and John and Anne shared the other. Even though the chancre sores and the fevers and rashes and all the other apparent symptoms of the infection had subsided, John did not wish to be intimate with his now six-month pregnant wife. It was late at night, and he did crave for some emotional intimacy. He didn't want to lay on top of her stomach, so he pulled her down on top of him. He began to kiss her first a little and then a lot. He could feel her heart pounding with fear. He looked at her face in the candlelight. Their noses were very close to each other, no more than an inch apart. As John starred into Anne's eyes equally with both of his, focusing on hers with equal strength suddenly her face took on a different appearance. Her head appeared as the shape of a pyramid, and the eyes emerged as only one, one eye in the middle of the pyramid-shaped head.

At first, he was afraid that this was a vision, but then he realised this was an optical illusion caused by the distance in space between humans' binocular eyes. He was later comforted by this pyramid with the all-knowing eye. For surely this meant that anyone that appears before you in this form already knows what you are thinking, they can see straight into your soul. John almost talked, but Anne said, "Shhhhh, I married you under the witness of God and I will be true to you under his continuing watch until the day you die."

They kissed again, and the pyramid with the eye vanished into the night.

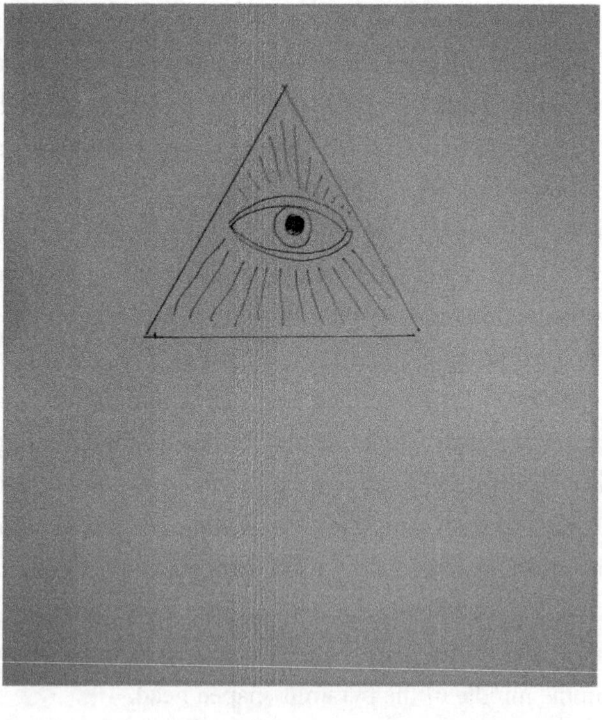

Masonic Symbol

On October 3rd, 1888, the decomposing torso was found. It was a slap on the face or the hand more appropriately, to the police department of Scotland Yard. The office was in a complete frenzy. Sir Charles Warren did understand the Masonic encoded messages to be careful with any accusations as there is alleged royal involvement with this case. The real killer had now officially set up a communication line with the head of the entire London Police Department. When the graffiti on the Wentworth building was discovered over the bloodied, and faecal-covered piece of the apron, Thomas Arnold, the Superintendent of the H division, had the chalk washed away before sunrise as he feared the writing might incite a religious riot. Arnold received so much criticism for doing such a thing with the only piece of hard evidence gathered until this point that he left the force the next day.

The Inspector in Charge of Detectives on the ground, drafted from the home office, was Frederick Abberline. The Chief Superintendent of the City of London Police Department (Scotland Yard) was Alfred Lawrence Foster. A few of the top officials had already left on sick leave due to the stress from the nature of the crimes and the inability to obtain a credible suspect.

Jack the Ripper had been born

The newspapers had already printed the 'Dear Boss' letter. The world was introduced to its very first official serial killer, and the police department now was faced with zero evidence after six brutal murders within two months. Sir Charles Warren opened communication with the Prime Minister and the Queen. There was some suggestion of possible involvement of Prince Eddie, but as he always had a good alibi, they were not sure that it was the result of the letter sent to the Queen threatening to tell about the Prince's alleged charge of rape. So the Queen instructed the Prime Minister to instruct the Chief of Police to proceed with the investigation as if he were 'walking on glass'.

Alfred L. Foster, the Superintendent of the City Police who was in charge of hundreds of men and hundreds more that were to be recruited just for the Whitechapel area, took the insult of the torso the hardest. He felt like a failure, but Mr Foster had a son, Frederick William Foster, who also worked at the City of London Police Department. The son, or Frederick Junior, was the architect/surveyor for the police force. His father, who had been on the force for a very long time, was a hardened veteran and he would not succumb to so much stress that he too would have to resign. However, he was grooming his son to be the head of the New Scotland Yard upon his retirement. The son, Frederick William Foster, was the one responsible for drawing the murder victims as they were found: their clothes, their positioning and their appearance; this was superimposed onto the architectural drawings of the environment of the surrounding area. Fredric Foster was further responsible for plotting the murder sites superimposed on a large map of Whitechapel to study possible escape routes or measure distances, located gas lamp lighting, underground railway paths, underground entrances, construction sites and other possibilities.

Foster felt even more compelled than Abberline from the (Criminal Investigation Department) as he wanted not only to defend his father's honour but to prove himself as the best detective in the greatest detective agency in the world. He wanted to be the head of the New Scotland Yard.

Foster set up his work around his office. He pinned up maps and plotted the distances and poured and poured over all of his drawings and notes. He knew all of the victims by name and had a mental list in his mind of each.

#1 Martha Tabram Aug 7th 1888 early a.m.
#2 Mary Ann Nichols Aug 31st 1888 early am
#3 Annie Chapman Sept 8th 1888 early am
#4 Elizabeth Stride Sept $30^{th,}$ 1888 early am
#5 Catherine Eddowes Sept $30^{th,}$ 1888 early am
#6 Oct 3rd 1888, unidentified torso

Foster stayed up for three nights straight and then suddenly, on the night of October 6th, he realised where he might have missed a clue. When Catherine Eddowes was murdered and found in Mitre Square, he didn't do the drawings at the scene. Foster had been dispatched and showed up around 3:30 am or so, but the body had been taken away at least an hour prior. When he then went to the morgue to at least draw the victim as she looked, even though she had been transported, he arrived only to find the body had already been stripped and cleaned. So Foster had to make his drawing of the victim not by how she now looked all cleaned up but by Dr Brown's quick sketch of his discovery of the body at the crime scene.

Foster stared at his wording of the survey specifically the words:

Drawn from a sketch taken at the mortuary by Mr F. W. Foster 3:45 A.M. Sunday, Sept 30th, 1888.

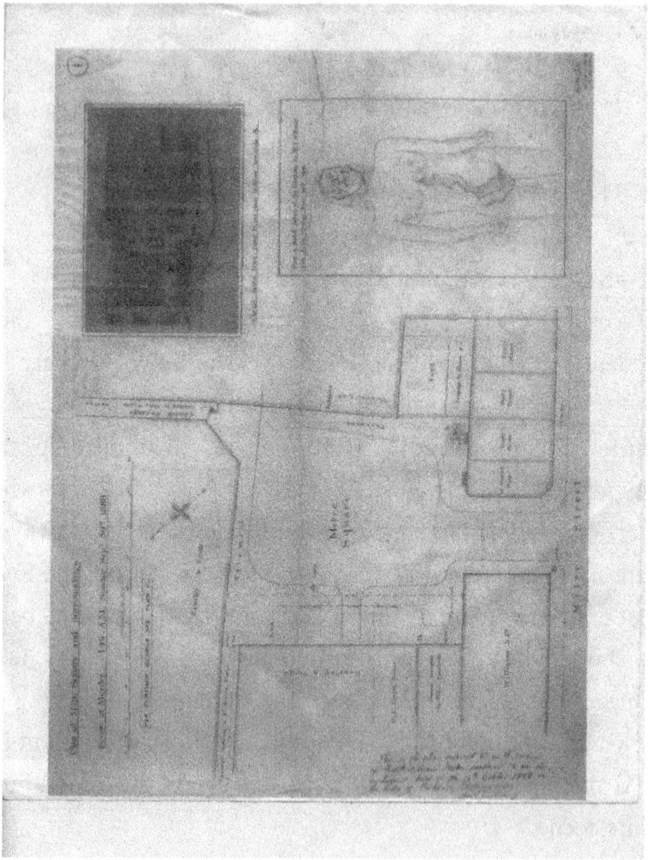

Chapter 15

Scotland Yard Steps up Its Game

Foster realised something might have been missed, but it was too late to go back and examine the body personally or the clothing for that matter. So, he requested a copy of the written notes that Dr Brown had made. And then Foster recreated this onto a large piece of paper on his drafting table. He focused on the doctor's description of the 'picking' of the eyes with the knife, the ear that was cut off, the intestines over the right shoulder and an approximate two-foot piece of intestine wedged under the left arm. Foster didn't know what this message meant but he knew it was some message. Then he focused on the doctor's further description of the facial wounds.

Two incisions on each cheek that formed symmetrical triangular flaps with a cut through the bridge of the nose.

Foster transferred this into a drawing and realised his killer had left him a clue 'M'. Frederick W. Foster went and summoned the help of his father, Alfred L Foster who lived in a flat next door to the police station at #26 Old Jewry Road. He ran next door and pounded on the door until his father woke up. Frederick Foster asked, "Father, I've come up with something; look at this drawing, do you know what it means?"

His father replied, "It means the murderer is either a freemason or familiar with the teachings. That means our Jack the Ripper is no dummy. It also means he's not Jewish."

Frederick Foster further inquired, "But what exactly in the freemason society does this portray?"

Foster Sr. continued, "It's an indication that the person who was slaughtered that way was a traitor."

Foster thanked his father and then went back to his drafting table. He sat there staring at his drawing with her bowels out and the 'M' on her face, with her ear half cut off. He kept asking out loud to himself, "*Who were you, Catherine? Talk to me? Tell me about yourself?*"

Then he suddenly had a thought, *Draw what she looked like when she was alive.*

He drew her body without her face all cut up and her guts hanging out. Then he wanted to recreate what she was wearing so he took out the list that described the clothes and drew them as he read the description:

* *Black straw bonnet trimmed in green and black velvet with black beads. Black strings, worn tied to the head.*

* *Black cloth jacket trimmed around the collar and cuffs with imitation fur and around the pockets in black silk braid and fur. Large metal buttons.*

* *Dark green chintz skirt, three flounces, the brown button on the waistband. The skirt is patterned with Michaelmas daisies and golden lilies.*

* *Man's white vest, matching buttons down the front*

* *Brown linsey bodice, black velvet collar with brown buttons down the front*

* *Gray stuffed petticoat with white waistband*

** Very old green alpaca skirt (worn as undergarment)*

** Very old ragged blue skirt with red flounces, light twill lining (worn as undergarment)*

** White calico chemise*

** No drawers or stays*

** Pair of men's lace-up boots, mohair laces. Right boot repaired with red string*

** 1 piece of red gauze silk worn as a neckerchief*

** 1 large white pocket handkerchief*

** 2 unbleached calico pockets, tape strings*

** 1 blue stripe bed ticking pocket*

** Brown ribbed knee stockings, darned with white cotton*

When Foster completed his drawing, he took one look at it and instantly had a recollection. She was the lady sitting in the middle of the station last Saturday precisely one week ago. He remembered looking at her as he passed by to go on his lunch break.

She stood out like a sore thumb, poor little thing. What did she know? What was she doing at the police station anyway?

He quickly went over to the record department and pulled last Saturday's requests. He looked down a short list of record requests. And his eyes were focused on the 'M' in Malthouse. He looked up the name of the clerk who had researched the record. It was too late at night to wake up the clerk, and if he was now hot on the trail of the killer, he didn't want to give the credit away. He wanted to figure it all out by himself. He would be a hero. So, Foster went and pulled the 1881 census for John Richard Malthouse. There were two; that was a problem. John Richard Malthouse the Fireman age 36, and John Richard Malthouse the soldier age 37. It seemed only logical to Foster that the fireman was the one that had something to do with the murders because the murder happened very close to the fire station where John Richard Malthouse, the fireman, was stationed. The murder happened in Mitre Square. Foster reviewed his drawing. Mitre Square had three entrances, or exits, one which leads to the main thoroughfare, one which leads to down St James Place, toward the fire station and the small footpath, cut through to the church. Then Foster began to think.

The victim, I'll call her Catherine now, Catherine was seen by three Jewish men talking at the crossroads of the pass that leads to the church with a man. Then Catherine was found murdered in the square that goes from the church to the fire station. Let me suppose here for a minute that the fireman, I'll call him John, was working the night shift and went on his break, he ran into this woman in the square, and he murdered her. But why did John kill her and display her body in such a way as to indicate she was a traitor? What did she say to him? Or better yet what did she hear or see him doing? That's what happened! She saw him and heard him doing something of much importance, that's why he cut at her eyes and cut off her ear. She was probably standing at the corner on the inside of the court, and he was just on the outside of the path. Maybe he had just killed a woman, the unidentified torso, and she overheard. No, no, none of that happened, what am I thinking. I forgot all about the first murder that happened that night. The fireman could not possibly have done the first murder then run back to kill this woman and then return to his post.

If I check tomorrow and the fireman was at his post, then it must not have been he that was the murderer. But the murderer signed his initials on her face, 'M'. Maybe she only knew the name John Richard Malthouse, and she was in the process of heading up to the fire station to see him when another man with the last name of 'M' attacked her and killed her. Oh, this doesn't make any sense I better wait until the morning when I can ask the clerk what he remembers about her. My brains are not going to figure this out tonight.

He then lay down and tried to sleep. But he couldn't sleep, he lay there thinking up various possible scenarios; then he recalled having read the doctor's notes that Catherine had a large bruise between her thumb and her finger on the left hand. Foster realised, *That's what would occur if someone had you in a thumb grip and was twisting your thumb up as a form of torture to get you to say something. That's it; he got what he needed to know out of her. She told him, and then he killed her. But what did she tell him?*

Foster got back up out of bed he couldn't stand it. Then he read the contents of her pockets:

* *2 small blue bags made of bed ticking*
* *2 short black clay pipes*
* *1 tin box containing tea*
* *1 tin box containing sugar*
* *1 tin matchbox, empty*
* *12 pieces of white rags*
* *1 piece of blue and white shirting, three-cornered*
* *1 piece red flannel with pins and needles*

** 6 pieces soap*

** 1 small tooth comb*

** 1 white handle table knife*

** 1 metal spoon*

** 1 red leather cigarette case with white metal fittings*

** 1 ball hemp*

** 1 piece of the white apron with repair*

** Several buttons and a thimble*

** Mustard tin containing two lottery tickets, one in the name of Emily Burrell, 52 White's Row, dated August 31st, 9d for a man's flannel shirt. The other is in the name of Jane Kelly of 6 Dorset Street and dated September 28th, 2S for a pair of men's boots.*

** Printed handbill*

** Portion of a pair of spectacles*

** 1 red mitten*

Bloody hell, Foster thought. *Kate, you were a ripe walking store!*

Then Foster focused on the lottery tickets.

Why did you have somebody else's lottery ticket that could have been cashed in over a month ago, that's because she only just gave it to you. But why didn't she cash it herself if she lived here in London also? And why didn't you cash in your lottery ticket? Let's face it you were both poor, love. I'm sure you really could have used those clothes. My God, look at what you were wearing Kate. Probably everything you owned. That's it, you were wearing everything you owned, and you didn't cash in those tickets, and your friend didn't either because you were away on vacation. You're too poor *for a vacation. You were off on another job. What kind of job were you and this other poor woman doing? August 31st through September 28th. September what can you do in September. Of course, that's the hop-picking season, isn't it? But the season lasts for five weeks it was still going on. Why did you race back here before the season was over? The autopsy shows you weren't sick Kate. You didn't race back home to cash in the lottery tickets because you weren't killed until September 30th and you hadn't cashed in the tickets yet. That's because you had something more pressing on your mind, didn't you dear? That's why you were in our office.*

Foster then pulled out the file on questioning boyfriend and skimmed through it.

Let's see here. Your boyfriend was John Kelly, and he thought your real name was Catherine Conway. You lived together for seven years. You were hop-picking in Hunton near Maidstone, you wanted to come home, you wouldn't go on with the other couple blah, blah, blah. No fight but wouldn't stay the night with him. He ran into you; you said you were going to look for your daughter in Bermondsey. But we both know that was a lie because you were in our office Saturday and you found out something and wanted to do a little checking on it and didn't want John to know even though you considered him your husband, you used his last name for seven years. The only thing that would make you do all that is because you were a greedy little woman, weren't you? You didn't want John to know what you were up to. Where did you stay that night? Let's see, um oh here John said you wanted to stay at the casual ward in Shoe Lane Mile's end because it wouldn't cost anything, you knew the deputy, and he would let you have the bed for free. I'm going to go to the Shoe Lane Lodging house and see whether he let you have the bed for free. I don't believe that, Deary.

Then he headed out the door for Mile's End. Even though it was now early am on Sunday, October 7th, Foster wanted to catch the night deputy. Foster arrived at the casual ward and began striking up a conversation with Fred the night deputy.

"I'm in charge of investigating the murder of Catherine Eddowes; her boyfriend said she stayed the night here the Friday before last night, just over a week ago. I've got a drawing here I made of what she looked like."

He produced his drawing of her in the clothes.

Fred said, "Oh, sure I remember her. She's the one that said she'd come back straight from hop-picking to claim the reward. She said she knows the murderer and I told her to be careful, and she said not to worry about that. Is that why she got murdered?"

Fred quickly said, "Evidently so, the poor stupid thing must have confronted him herself. It got her killed huh? Too bad she didn't tell anyone who he was first. It would be pretty hard to get her to tell us from the grave huh? Yeah, you're right. She didn't tell me his name."

Foster thanked him for his cooperation and then added: "What did you charge her for the night?"

Fred replied, "Two pence."

Then Foster left and waved goodbye. He began mumbling to himself, "I knew he wouldn't give you a bed for free, you didn't want your husband to know that you were going to discover the murderer so you could get all that money yourself."

By the time he arrived back at the police station, the clerk who looked up the records for Kate was there at the desk again. Foster acted very coolly and calmly, he could taste that promotion coming already.

Foster asked the clerk, "Can you get me the record of last week's searches?"

The clerk quickly pulled out the clipboard and asked, "What day?"

"The Saturday before last, September 29th," Foster replied. The clerk then flipped to the requests for the day.

Foster then asked, "Is there a request for a John Richard Malthouse?"

The clerk looked at the shortlist and said, "Yeah right here."

Foster played dumb, "Who requested it?"

"It says Jane Kelly, his cousin," replied the clerk.

"Does it say why?"

The clerk replied, "No, it doesn't say why, but I can tell you because I was the one that researched it. A poor pauper wanted to know where her cousin lived now; she said she hadn't seen him for a long time and was worried about him, why are you asking?"

Foster quickly said, "I saw a woman yesterday outside the fire station, she was drunk and disorderly; when I questioned her and thought about arresting her, she claimed she was so excited that she found her long-lost cousin, John Richard Malthouse that she couldn't contain herself. She added that she had had to come over here to our station to look him up. I believed her, and so I let her go. I was checking back to make sure she wasn't telling me a fib."

The clerk added, "No, she wasn't fibbing. She must have been worried about him because she sat right over there for at least four hours waiting for me to look him up. She said he hadn't shown up at the Malthouse hop-picking family reunion, and that's why she was so worried. The only thing I thought was odd is that she didn't even know how old he was. She referred to his age by saying his wife was about ten years younger than herself. I'm glad she finally found him though."

"Yeah, me too," replied Foster. "I guess we're all allowed to get a little drunk over something like that."

Then Foster left the front desk and went upstairs to his quarters. He sat down and put some facts down on a piece of paper.

#1 Kate hop picking in Kent

#2 Finds out something and races home to check out John Richard Malthouse

#3 Doesn't know John Richard Malthouse personally

#4 Knows John's wife or at least has seen John's wife because makes reference to wife's approximate age.

#5 *Wants the reward money and doesn't want anyone else to know what she knows because she wants the money all to herself. So, she lies every time someone comes close to finding out what she's up to.*

Then Foster wrote out:

Hypothetical situation: There was a Malthouse family reunion, and she overheard a conversation which explicitly indicated a real credible doubt as to whether or not he was the murderer. The accusation probably came from his wife.

Conclusion: The John Richard Malthouse whose wife was just hop-picking in Kent is the murderer.

Foster quickly headed out the door again for the #23 St Botolph's Bishopsgate Fire station. When he arrived there, he found three firefighters on duty.

Foster casually asked, "John's not here, right? He works the night shift, doesn't he?"

One of the firemen replied, "Yeah, he'll be back on tonight, why do you ask?"

Foster replied, "Oh, it's not him I wanted to talk to, it's his wife. Is she here?"

Another fireman said, "No, she's probably down at the market, that's where she hangs out."

Foster said, "I work for the police, and I got a request from a cousin of hers wondering why she didn't show up for the Malthouse hop-picking family reunion, they wanted me to check and see if she was okay."

Then one of the firemen said, "I don't know why she didn't go, maybe she didn't get the invitation. I'll ask her?"

Foster asked, "Was she around here last month or did she not go because she went on vacation somewhere else?"

The fireman replied, "No, she was around here all last month."

Foster said, "Oh, you know what, don't ask her why she didn't go, maybe she didn't want to go. Maybe she doesn't like her in-laws or something. Don't embarrass her, don't even tell her I was here. I'll just let her family know she's all right. Thanks, guys," and then Foster left.

He went back to his office and sat back down at his drafting table, leaned back and said:

Okay, Johnny boy, or should I call you Jack. I'm going to become your new shadow. I'm going to know everything there is to know about you. You must be one damn smart guy to kill poor Kate just before she made it to the fire station. Ten minutes or even five minutes later and she would have made it there, and you'd get caught. Damn it, Kate. Five minutes faster. Why didn't you run? How did he find out about you and how did he get to you. You weren't even a prostitute. How did he get to you? He befriended you, didn't he? He gained your trust. It wasn't he that put you in the thumb squeeze, was it? It was probably your husband John trying to make you tell him what you were up to. No Jack's not the type to use a thumb squeeze, he just played you along. Oh, Jack. I'm getting excited now; I'm going to get to you. I'm going to know you without you ever even being tipped off. I sure can't let you know I'm questioning your wife. I'd probably wind up as a torso. I'm going to have to befriend your wife myself. I'm going to become your wife's secret lover.

Foster went down to the records department and made sure nobody knew what he was doing. Foster looked things up and jotted them down his notes.

John Richard Malthouse:

Born in Brighton Dec 3rd, 1851 – no record of christening – (? Bastard)

Joined 10th Royal Prince Albert's own Hussars at age 18, in 1869 – (? Who sponsored it)

Deployment India, Afghanistan, Canterbury, Aldershot and now York

Awards – Afghan medal, best shot, best swordsman, fastest ¼ runner in India for 3 years in succession

Rank – Sargent Farrier/ Silversmith

Reported Mother to be Emily Malthouse who was born around 1839

Then Foster began to look up a file for Emily Malthouse and found the following:

Emily Malthouse:

Born? However, christened at Saint Nicholas church in Brighton Sept 27th, 1829

Parents – John and Mary (Sheehy) Malthouse, registered Quakers

No other listed siblings

No record of John or Mary Malthouse's death = (Quaker's buried unmarked graves?)

Emily didn't receive her parents' inheritance, she was not included in on will? Disownment?

Emily had a daughter Adelaide born at St George's Hanover Square in 1849. Emily claimed her own birthplace as London, not Brighton, or someone else did it for her?

1861 census for Emily Malthouse:

R.G. 9/101 Page 74 Parrish – St Pancras, Borough – Marylebone District – St John

Household Members:

Name Relation COND Age Occupation Birthplace

James Malthouse (head) Mar 24 Porter Brighton

Amelia Malthouse (wife) / 30 Bookbinder London

Adelaide Malthouse (daughter)13 St George's
James Law (visitor)????? UN 24 Porter St Pancras

1871 census for Emily Malthouse
R.G. 10 503 Book 77 Page 33 Parrish – Christchurch Borough – Spitalfields
Street Name – John Street #14
Household Members:
Name Relation Cond Age Occupation Birthplace
James Malthouse (head) Mar 36 Carsman Sussex Brighton
Adelaide Malthouse (wife) Mar 40 Dressmaker City of London
Emily Malthouse (daughter) Un 22 Machinist St George Hanover
John Carroll (visitor) ?????? Un 22 Carsman Surrey Lambeth

1881 mapped census for Buck's Row
1st building on list 'Malt House Cottage' Hosiers
Head – Edward Tipple: aged 29 – Born Suffolk –Manager of Hoosiers
Boarder – Charles Tipple: aged 27 – Born Suffolk – Outfitter's Clerk
Boarder – Frank Tipple: aged 18 – Born Suffolk – Upholsterers Clerk

Emily died in 1773 at St George Hanover Square listed as warden of the state, however, death certificate listed birthplace as Brighton again?

Foster then brought these notes upstairs and digested them for a while and then wrote:

Hypothesis: John's mother, Emily Malthouse, the only daughter of a rich Quaker couple gets pregnant and comes to London secretly and gives birth to Adelaide in 1848, then she leaves her daughter at a workhouse, and she goes back to Brighton where she gets pregnant again and has John Richard Malthouse in Brighton. Then she gets disowned from her parents for having a child out of wedlock. Becomes a pauper and stays at St George with Adelaide and... Where did John go? Foster family?

Then goes to St Pancras ends up in Whitechapel with James Malthouse that she claims is husband (relative? cousin?) John Richard Malthouse joins military 1868. Emily dies alone in 1873, buried in a pauper's grave at St George (daughter Adelaide didn't attend the funeral?) Daughter hated Mother for leaving her alone at St George after giving birth to her; son John Richard Malthouse hates Mother also. The murders are crimes of hatred for Mother, not crimes of a sexual nature.

#1 Mary Ann Nichols turns up dead right in front of Malt House Cottage

#2 Annie Chapman found killed in the backyard of the house where the owner is a widow named Emily and the son is called John, age 37, who lived on John Street

Foster took a deep breath and leaned back in his chair.

Okay John, you hate your mommy but who was your daddy? She was an educated, wealthy Quaker daughter; she wasn't some whore from the Eastend. Must it have been someone very compelling to make you risk disownment from the Quaker Church? And disownment from your parents who would have left you with a big fat inheritance? (Royal Involvement? Brighton Conception Royal Pavilion in 1848 with Emily? And at Isle of Wight in 1850, with John, because the Pavilion was abandoned in 1849). Of course, that's it, these records have probably already been altered or were altered at the time they were conducted to cover-up?

There was no cousin claiming to be Emily's husband, was there? You were the head of the household. Your mother never got married, and there was no James; that's why your mother is in a paupers' grave. Look at the dates and names of your mother and sister? They're inverted in the 1871 census. You did that to let me know these censuses were tampered with or inaccurate. And look at Malthouse Cottage in the 1881 census, it was a functional Hoosier even after your mother's death. Keep going.

Fred kept talking out loud.

Your mother died in 1873; that's when you went off to India. She died of a broken heart. She loved you, and she was never a whore. Maybe they killed her? Oh my God, that's it. The records have been altered you probably didn't join the army until she had died, at age 44? That's very young. At the hospital. Did one of the doctors kill her? Prince Albert kept her safe until he died in 1861, and you were ten years old, and then you took care of your mom and sister. You were your mom's protector until you went to India. They wanted to shut her up, once they knew you couldn't come to check on her anymore. You're just making someone think you hate your mother, and you're doing an excellent job at it!

Foster took out his map and then he plotted out the six murder sites all on the same map. He was an architect; he was used to measuring things and looking for perfectly square walls. He noticed that the murders between murder #2, 3 and 4 made a triangle. He measured with his compass.

Yes, it's very close to an isosceles triangle, he said to himself.

Foster's brain was now racing:

You're talking to me, I mean you are talking directly to me. What are you telling me? Okay, let me think about this. You're letting me know where the next murder is going to be aren't you? Murder #7. Seven is an extraordinary number, isn't it? Let me review this. I'll call the victims by their number and not their name; this will be easier because they all give different names all the time.

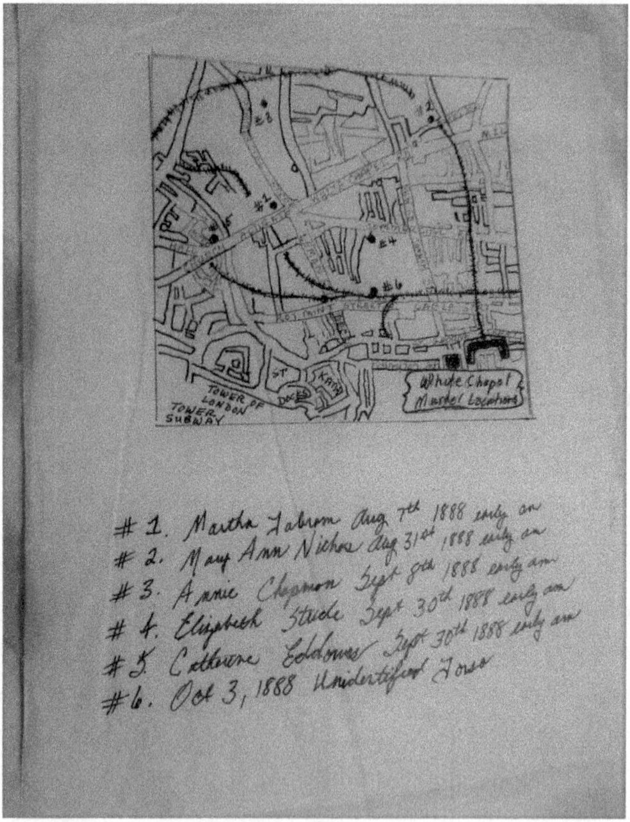

#1 = You're letting me know you were a soldier and you got fucked. (Witnesses saw the victim with soldier and sex took place.)

#2 =Your name is Malthouse (The body was dumped in front of 'Malthouse' cottage)

#3 =Your mom is named Emily with no husband and you, being the 37-year-old son lived on John Street (During the time of the murder, a widow, Emily Richardson lived there;

her son, John Richardson, who was also 37 years old lived on John Street)

#4 ??????? It must have a reference to where #7 will be. I know she's the pinpoint to the next triangle.

#6 didn't count she didn't have a head or much of anything else; she was just a symbol of you snubbing Scotland Yard.

Then Foster measured the distance between #4 and #5 and approximated its isosceles point around Dorset Street.

Okay, what was that silly wall message again?

The Jewes are the men that should not be blamed for nothing

You mean the Jewess or female traitor is not the one to be blamed, the men are the ones to be blamed. Which men? Which men, John? Oh, of course, the torso was found next #6 Scotland Yard or the police are to be blamed. You've been talking to me all this time in a code that I think is Masonic. Are you trying to tell all the masons what is going on or are you trying to say to me they too are the men to blame? That would mean Sir Charles Warren, and who else? I don't think my dad ever did become a mason? Maybe he is, I better find out. Tell me some more Jack. Tell me some more.

#3 her intestines were around her shoulders but not that deliberately. She wasn't a traitor. An envelope was found, up by her head. It had two pills in it, it had the royal seal and an M and then a 2 and then an Sp. 2 pills John? For what Sp I get it = Syphilis. And the M is for Malthouse. You or your mom, John, which one? Or is it an "M" for the next victim's Name? #3 Was also found with two farthings at her feet.

Foster took out two farthings. They were found head up. He read what they said, *Okay, 'Brittania' 2 farthings, 'Brittania' 2 farthings, 'Brittania'. That means safe passage. You give two farthings to the gatekeeper, or the ferryman or something like that, for safe passage into the land of the dead. Okay, safe passage for who? When?*

Foster looked at his calendar. *She was killed on Saturday, November 8th. When's the next eighth? Foster looked at the month of November. Thursday, November 8th, that's the day before Prince Albert Edwards's birthday. She is supposed to be killed as a birthday gift to him because she, 'M', got syphilis from someone, we can assume it's Edward's son, Victor who has that reputation. The last victim #6, we won't count anymore, her name that she reported to the police before she was killed was 'Mary Kelly'. The officer who released her from jail that night said, she said, her name was 'Mary Kelly'. Mary Kelly is the name of the girl you want to save from getting killed.*

Where was that package found again?

Foster plotted the outhouse package. It was in the very centre of London, Kentish Town on Victoria Road.

You're telling me shit on Victoria and shit on London and shit on England. That's why there was shit on the bloody apron. So the Jewess is Victoria. Shit on Victoria and shit on the men in London or England that do the covering up for Royalty.

Okay, I get it, Jack. You are making double codes, aren't you? You're making the Royalty think you're doing their dirty work. You're making the freemasons assume you are doing their dirty work, but you're double-crossing them. You're are going to give free passage to the next victim on Thursday, November 8th at the Brittania Pub on Dorset Street, and you want my help, and I can't tell anyone else. Oh, why me Jack? Why did you pick me? I know it's because I'm the smartest and probably the only trustworthy one here, right? Okay, Jack, I believe you. You've got my help. I'll be there waiting for her. I won't tell anybody — not even my father.

Foster then threw all his notes, everything he had into the fireplace at the station.

Sickert had bought a small box of about three inches square in diameter. He put the piece of the kidney in it which had been sitting in his wine glass all that time. And then he mailed it off to Mr Lusk. Mr Lusk received it on October 16th. The kidney was immediately sent to a medical examiner who concluded that it probably was, in fact, a piece of a diseased kidney as the deceased had Blight's disease, a disease of the kidney caused from drinking too much gin, and the portion of the kidney that was sent also appeared in the same manner. Sickert was exhilarated with so much attention to his wonderful poems being printed all over the newspapers that he immediately wrote up another one. This time Sickert decided to send it to the medical examiner:

Dr Oppenshaw

Old boss, you was rite it was the left kidny I was goin to hoperate agin close to your ospitle just as I was going to dror mi nife along of er bloomin throte them cusses of coppers

spoilt the game but I guess I wil be on the job soon and will send you another bit of innerds
Jack the Ripper

O have you seen the devle
With his mikerscope and scalpul
A –lookin at a kidney
With a slide cocked up

The letter was received on October 29th, 1888.

However, the letter never found its way to the newspapers. A message was delivered telling Sickert to get in touch with Mary. Sickert headed down to the Brittania pub and waited all day. He was getting frustrated that Mary always woke up late. Finally, he saw her and motioned her over to him.

"Mary, do you remember red right ha ha? Red right ha ha?" Sickert didn't realise Mary was illiterate and therefore never could read the newspaper articles of the killings. She had her boyfriend, Barnett read her all of the articles, so she didn't understand the message because she never saw the underlined words from the first of the Jack the Ripper murder letters. So, Mary just thought Sickert was strange, but now she thought he was really strange.

Sickert continued, "I'm just a messenger, and I have a message for you."

Sickert then pulled a piece of paper out of his pocket and began to read it to Mary very slowly.

"The necessary investigations have been completed. At this point, we only want to take the baby, and we will leave you unharmed. We will give you 500 pounds for the exchange. We will get back in touch with you once you have had time to think about it."

Mary said, "What they're going to wait five more months then take the baby?"

Sickert said, "No Mary, don't you get it, they want to take the baby soon."

Mary looked at Sickert and then said, "Oh, now I understand. They want to take the baby?"

Sickert replied, "Yes Mary, they want to take the baby. I hope you don't TAKE too long to make a decision. I'm sure I'll be sent back soon for your answer."

Then Sickert quickly stood up and pulled his hat down over his eyes and bent over out of people's view and then he quickly walked away and rode the underground back to his studio.

Mary went home that evening and discussed with her boyfriend, Joseph Barnett, who had been living with her for the past eight months. She told him that she was sure by now that he realised that she was pregnant for the last four months. She told him that she was thinking about having the baby aborted. Joe got very upset with the suggestion. Mary had never told him about Prince Eddie, the rape, or the bribery because she wanted the money all to herself. He thought the baby was his. At the thought of that, Barnett told her that all the other whores that she had been letting stay there with them had corrupted her mind. He gathered together his things on that October 30th and moved out of their #13 Room at Miller's Court, Dorset Street and moved to 24-25 Buller's Boarding House, New Street Bishops Gate. After Barnett moved out, Mary continued to let one lady share the room with her.

Back at Scotland Yard, Foster had convinced his father, the Superintendent, that it might be good for him also to go undercover against the Whitechapel murders. He told his father he would take up the identity of a Mr Hutchinson and take out a place at the Victoria Home on Commercial Street and blend in with the neighbourhood. His father agreed it sounded like a good idea. Foster picked this name for a particular reason. During the questioning of the three Jewish men that were leaving the Imperial Club on the night of the double murder, one of the witnesses hinted to the police that he might have recognised the killer as a man who lived on Buck's Row. He was too afraid to say more than that. His name was Mr Levy. However, his butcher shop was at Hutchinson's Street for the last thirty-six years. Foster was sure that John was a bit worried about this witness, as he could identify him. So Foster set up camp in Whitechapel. He hung out at the Brittania and quickly met Mary Kelly or Dark Mary as she frequently called herself. He befriended Mary by frequently giving her doss money; he also suggested it was safer, and cheaper to keep a roommate.

John was back in York and discussed the plan for Mary's murder with Eddie who said he had nothing scheduled for the whole month of November but that he was going to Sandringham in December from the second through the twelfth. John agreed that would be enough time. Then they planned the murder. John asked Dr Gull to come over and so the three talked. John told Dr Gull: "Eddie came up with the great plan back at Sickert's. We trick Mary Kelly into thinking we are going to perform an abortion on her and then she'll hand over the button, and we'll give her the five hundred pounds."

Eddie jumped in, "I guess I never corrected the little button issue. You see it wasn't my button that whore pulled off my shirt it was my Prince of Wales Plumes with my name engraved on the back. I guess I was too into it to notice; she was playing so hard to get anyway. I love it when they fight but not when they steal my pin! Anyway, what were you saying? Oh yeah, my idea about a pretend abortion. I love it when I come up with such good ideas."

John turned to Dr Gull and said, "That's why I wanted you here. The women of Whitechapel are now terrified. Mary is going to be suspicious of me unless I have a great disguise. I want to borrow your doctor's bag and be introduced before my arrival as the royal doctor, Doctor Gull."

Dr Gull's eyes lit up with excitement as he quickly remarked: "That's a brilliant idea. Here let me give you my bag."

Then he opened the bag up. It had a full set of instruments which included very sharp knives. John picked through a couple of the knives and tested their sharpness. He wasn't satisfied.

"Before I fillet her, I would like to sharpen these tools a little if you don't mind. But tell me doctor, which instruments would one use if one were to do a real abortion?"

Dr Gull loved his medicine and loved the opportunity to teach. He excitedly said, "I will be performing an induced delivery on one of the ladies probably next week. If you pretend to be my assistant, you can watch. Have you any medical experience?"

"Yes," replied John, "a bit. I'm the farrier, so I do all the surgical assisting with the animals; both with or without the veterinarian's assistance. I've delivered a lot of foals. And many times on the battlefield, I've been the only one left alive in good enough shape to provide medical care to the men. I've done some amputations, sutures and mercy killings."

Dr Gull clapped his hands and said, "This is going to be so great. But don't do a mercy killing on her; you're going to ram your knife so hard up that whore's vagina and uterus that it should cut right through her intestines and she's going to be laying out spread eagle waiting for you to do it. I wish I could be there to watch."

Then Eddie turned to John and said, "I don't want even one little clue that points my direction. This is my last communication with you until we do it. I hope you'll have my pin for me when I arrive on the twelfth; then I won't have to keep making excuses about my whereabouts. Finalise the arrangements yourself, with Sickert and Arthur, use your corporal again if you need someone to watch your back."

Then they all parted ways.

John sent a message to Sickert to get back in touch with Mary. He said, *Tell her this message exactly as the doctor told me he wanted it sent, he told me to tell you he wanted you to tell her this, so write it down. 'If you have decided to give up the baby, a carriage will be sent on the afternoon of Friday the seventh'.*

Then John sent a message to Arthur, *On the evening of November the seventh, I want you to go down to the Brittania Pub and look for our lady, Mary. She is about 5'5" and has beautiful blue eyes, long golden blond hair and fair skin; she's about twenty-five years old. She speaks with an Irish brogue even though sometimes she claims she's Welsh. The bartender should direct you toward her if you ask for 'Dark Mary'. Then quickly introduce yourself to Mary as the assistant to Dr Gull, the royal physician. Tell her right away that Walter Sicker has been arrested as the murderer. Tell her we became suspicious of him when he wanted to personally pick you up in a carriage that wasn't supposed to be the arrangement. We could never do this in a hospital because then there would be too many witnesses. Say the police were already suspicious of him because all of the victims had been his models, and that it appeared he was a little deranged. We apologise for using him as our messenger, but he was the only one we knew who could recognise her. Then she'll feel very comfortable with you. Buy her a pail of beer and bring it back to her room. Then tell her to drink half of it for an anaesthetic. Tell her that Dr Gull will be arriving sometime around 2:00 am as he was caught up in surgery at the London Royal Hospital. See if she'll give you the button first, but I doubt it, don't push her. Tell her she can give it to the doctor after the surgery when the doctor gives her 500 pounds. Then tell her to get a pot of water ready in the fireplace as we'll need boiling water to sterilise the towels. Once you're in the room, set up the furniture in such a way so I'll have good lighting to see what I'm doing. Set up the bed and a table beside it for my instruments. Whatever you do, don't spook her. Whatever she says, go along with it. I've seen you in action, Arthur; you're pretty quick on the draw. You're going to be the hero here. You're the man that talks the lamb into walking itself into the slaughterhouse. Then leave before midnight. I don't want you anywhere around there. We can't chance it that Lord Salisbury be in any way considered involved. I'll take it from midnight. Tell her the doctor will be waiting at the Queen's Head Pub. Describe my appearance to her and tell her to be on the lookout for me, Dr Gull, and that she can then lead me back to her room.*

Arthur understood and couldn't wait again for the opportunity to practice his acting skills. He kept looking through his wardrobe for an outfit that wasn't too fancy to make anyone recognise him as Lord Salisbury but not so shabby that he wouldn't appear as an assistant to a doctor. Arthur tried on outfit after outfit and finally settled with a dark suit, a dark coat and a round, hard billy-cock hat. Then he put the clothes in the wardrobe in anticipation of his big debut. John had all his ducks in a row, and he went back to the barrack to be with his wife.

Anne went into labour on November third. John was there with her and Anne's mother, Elizabeth. The midwife sent John out of the room while the delivery actually took place and as soon as the baby was cleaned up and Anne was not exposed, John was called back in to hold his new baby son. They held off on the name as the last four sons had died soon after birth. John held the baby in his arms and then slowly watched his colour turn from pink to a shade of lavender and then dull grey and then bluish. He watched his son take his last little breath of air and then no more.

John knew deep down inside his sons were dying as penance for what he had done. He was being punished. John handed back over the dead infant to the nurse-midwife and said, "We have quit having funerals after our first son died, please take care of this for me and don't show it to Anne, it's too painful for her."

Anne went into depression again, but at least she had her mother there for comfort.

On the morning of November 6th, John left his grieving wife and headed to London. When he got to Spitalfields, he found that the deputy of Crossingham's, Donovan, had died sometime in November in the hospital from TB or pneumonia. John had not wanted to take a room back there because, on the night of the double murders, he never returned after paying for the place. He had since wondered if Donovan ever became suspicious of that, but now that he was dead and gone, John checked back into Crossinghams as it was the best location for the event. John got a room up on the second floor with a direct view of Mary's room.

Chapter 16

Prince Eddie's Birthday Gift - Mary's Heart

The next day Friday the seventh, Mary headed over to the pub at the Brittania; she sat there looking very nervous for a long time. Mr Hutchingson saw Mary in the bar looking nervous and asked what was wrong; Mary said it was a woman's problem and didn't want to discuss it with him. So, Mr Hutchingson introduced Mary to one of his close friends, Mrs Elizabeth Foster. He said he views her as close as his wife and that Mary could talk to her. Mary told Elizabeth Foster all about her worries of having an abortion, and Mrs Foster reassured her that everything would be all right. By 7:00 pm, when no carriage had arrived to take her to the hospital. Mrs Foster suggested that Mary go back to her room and make herself comfortable and that Mr Hutchingson would fetch her when the carriage arrives. Mary agreed and went back to her room. When Mary got to her room one of the prostitutes that occasionally stayed with Mary had let herself into the room through a break in the window that had been there for about four weeks. The break was near the door, and it was easy to reach in and unlock the latch.

All of Mary's friends had learned that. Mary and the woman ate dinner together there, as the woman brought enough for Mary in hope's that it would be in consideration for letting her stay the night. Mary agreed to let her wait there as Maria Harvey, the woman that most frequently stays with her, had not come back to check with Mary about staying for tonight. Then Barnett came in, and Mary told Barnett she was going to have an abortion that night. Barnett became very angry, but he couldn't talk Mary out of it. He stormed off and forgot his pipe. Mary got upset and decided to go back to the Brittania again and wait there. She still sat with Elizabeth Foster and drank beer while Mrs Foster continued to reassure her of everything. At 10:45 pm, Arthur showed up, he immediately picked out Mary sitting with Elizabeth Foster without having to ask the bartender and went over and asked to speak with her in private. They stepped outside, and he did as John had instructed him. He told her about Sickert being detained and how it was never supposed to be a carriage ride to a hospital and all the rest. Then he bought a pail of beer for Mary, and the two of them headed out of the pub. They reached Mary's room at 11:45 pm, just as she was about to enter the room with Arthur one of her neighbours, Mary Ann Cox, a fellow 31-year-old prostitute said goodnight to Mary. The prostitute had followed Mary all the way down the street as all the prostitutes tried to watch out for each other. She was letting Arthur know she was taking a good look at him. Mary sent a coded message back to the friend in a somewhat intoxicated voice she said, "Good night, I am going to sing."

Then she brought Arthur inside and they set up the room.

Mary put a kettle of water over the fireplace and had the fire ready to be lit. John was right; she wouldn't give the button to Arthur.

"Not until it was over," said Mary.

Then Arthur told her what the Doctor looked like and said to meet him at the Queen's Head Pub at around 2:00 am. Then Arthur left just before midnight. And Mary sang 'A Violet from Mother's Grave', and she sang and sang and sang. Some neighbours were ready to shout shut up by then. Mary then headed over to the Queen's Head Pub but just before she went inside John tapped her on the back. John looked very official; he was wearing a grey felt hat and a long dark coat trimmed in Astrakhan. He had a white collar with a black necktie pinned with a horseshoe pin, dark spats over light button boots and a massive gold chain with a large seal with a red stone on it. He carried kid gloves in his left hand and Dr Gull's bag in his right hand.

John said, "You must be Mary Kelly. My assistant came back to the hospital just when I was finishing up and told me everything was set up. Is that correct?"

Mary was convinced that John was the royal physician (Dr Gull). She did not recognise him as the man that watched her while she looked pleadingly at him when Prince Eddie raped her.

She said: "Yes, everything is ready."

John then reassured Mary, "I have a lot of experience with this type of procedure, you will be okay, I assure you." And then Mary led John back to her room. Mary put on the fire as instructed and began to boil some water. John told Mary, "You will need to take off all your clothes from your waist downward and anything else that you don't want to get blood on."

And then John watched as Mary slowly got undressed. She took the time to fold each article of clothing as she took it off and placed them on a table. And then she laid down on the bed that was moved caddy corner to the fire. John set out all the instruments from the bag onto a small nightstand that Arthur had positioned at the foot of the bed. Then John pulled over a chair toward the bottom of the bed and said, "You will need to bend your knees and scoot all the way down to the bottom of the bed."

Once Mary had scooted down, John recalled how he painted her so many months ago, how he stood to appreciate the beauty of her naked body. How beautifully her long golden hair which reached her waist lied in waves around her breast; how the candles had flickered about her dancing lights upon her curves. Her skin was as white and perfect and fair as no other skin could be. And how clean and beautifully she smelled.

Then John told her, "Now spread your legs until your knees rest on the sides of the bed." John slowly pushed aside her red pubic hair until he could visualise her labia. Then with his left hand, he pulled apart her labia and inserted his right hand two fingers deep inside her vagina. He pushed all the way in until he could feel her cervix. Then he took his left hand and began to push on the outside of her lower abdomen while pushing in her vagina hard with his right hand. He could feel a lump inside her womb. She was pregnant.

John said, "You're about five months pregnant, my dear. Are you sure you want to go through with it?"

Mary then said, "Oh yes, I do. I would never want to bring a child into this world that had him for a father. The child would probably grow up with mental problems from his lousy blood or be born with his sickness. I am sure I don't want this child to be born, but please do it quickly as I am losing my nerve."

John then saw Mary's legs shaking uncontrollably.

"Mary, why don't you get back up and have some more of that beer from the pail. Give me the button so that if you get so drunk and you pass out, I won't have to wait until you come through to get it. I will leave the money on your mantel and leave you there to sleep. Is there a way for me to let myself out and still lock the door? Do you have a key hidden somewhere?"

Mary replied, "I've lost the key, we reach in the window over there behind the coat that is hanging over the window. You can reach the latch easily that way. And the button is over here;" she reached into a little cupboard that was hanging on the wall. She pushed one of the jars aside and handed the button to John. He looked at the Prince of Wales plumes pin with the Prince's initials engraved on them and said: "You realise this is no 'button', don't you?"

Mary said, "I know."

And then she went over and poured some more beer and sat down on the bed and talked with John. Mary had not wanted to get any of her clothes soiled not even her bodied undergarment, so she was completely naked sitting beside John in front of the fire. As she drank, she told John she hated the life she led. She told him of how she used to be a lady, and travel around France in fancy clothes. And that it was an awful life that she had fallen into. She was going to take the 500 pounds and catch a ferry back to Ireland. She would return to her family, a family that knew nothing of the horrible life she was now living.

"I am going to be born again," Mary said, "This is my one opportunity for a second chance at life."

She said 'Bottoms up' and swigged down the rest of the beer, including a ginger beer that she had brought back with her the first time she left Elizabeth Foster. Then she laid back down on the bed and scooted to the bottom and spread her legs all the way open in front of John. This time her legs weren't shaking. John took out a few rags and poured the boiling water onto them. Then he laid his instruments out onto one of the clean cloths and wiped over them with another. Taking out the speculum and with his left hand, he gently spread apart her labia and with his right hand, he inserted a speculum. He opened the speculum as wide as possible. Mary flinched but didn't let out a sound. He took his right hand and reached all the way into her vagina with his whole hand; he felt her cervix, it felt like the end of a sausage, and then he forced one finger into the centre of it. After one finger was in, he pushed in another and once both fingers were in he forced his third finger and then twisted them in a circular motion thus stripping all of her membranes, Mary moaned a little.

Then John, not wanting to insert a knife and cut up the foetus, he removed the speculum. Then he reached in with his whole right arm he forced his hand through her now enlarged cervix and felt the foetus. He pulled it out of her while she moaned in pain. It came out still attached to its umbilical cord John held it in his hand. It was a tiny perfect boy, but too tiny to live. He held it in his left hand. Then John reached back into Mary's vagina with his right hand and felt the placenta he pulled off as much as he could that the umbilical cord was still attached to. Then he dropped the placenta to the floor and held the small baby in his hands. His hands were cupped together as it was small enough to fit in them.

Then the door opened up, and a lady walked in, she saw all the blood on the bed and Mary lying on the bed still and lifeless, she saw John sitting at the bottom of the bed she let out a scream.

"Oh, murder!"

And then Mary said, "I'm not dead, don't worry."

The lady felt so faint that she sat down on one of the chairs and leaned back. Then a man came through the door; it was Barnett. He had heard the scream of the lady as he had been hanging around Mary's apartment making sure she was okay. Barnett asked what was going on when he saw all the blood.

Mary told him, "He's the doctor. I just had an abortion." Barnett took one look at John as he was still cupping the foetus in his hands.

Barnet said, "A doctor would have done this in a hospital, he's not a doctor, look at him he's still cuddling our baby."

John then looked at him with a sick grin and held up a knife.

Barnett said, "He's the murderer, don't murder my Mary; she's sweet. Why don't you take this whore instead, she's the real whore."

Barnette had grabbed up the lady who was sitting on the chair and as the lady tried to yell Barnett muffled her scream with his hand held over her mouth.

Then John said, "If she's a whore, why don't you kill her?"

It was almost like a hypnotic suggestion to Barnett he couldn't stop himself. He smashed the lady's head against the wall three times, and she slid down the wall leaving a trail of blood.

"Now look what you've done," John said. "But I feel sorry for you. You lost your control; it's understandable. You loved Mary, and you thought I was going to kill her. You mistook me for the murderer. I will clean this up for you. But you can't say anything about me ever being here. Abortions are illegal you know. I will lose my license if anyone finds out I did an abortion. If you mention even one word about me, I will tell the police you were the murderer. Go home, tell the police you were playing cards or something like that. I will make this lady unrecognisable. Identify the body as that of Mary's. The police will think she was just another victim of Jack the Ripper. Mary, you put on that lady's clothes and leave, go to the Brittania Pub and wait for me. I will give you the money when I have finished here."

Mary got up off the bed an enormous amount of blood drained out of her vagina. Mary was in shock from the amount of blood loss. She was getting cold and trembling. John and Barnett pulled the clothes off of the lady and gave them to Mary who quickly put them on. Then John said, "LEAVE!"

And Mary and Barnett quickly left the room.

Then John swooped up the body and placed it on the bed; he felt her neck with his fingers. She had a good pulse. She had only been knocked out. John then took off all of his clothes and placed them safely in the corner of the room. John was now completely naked. Then John stood up straight and twisted his head quickly to the right and then slowly toward the left, he began to grunt like the sound of a racehorse in anticipation of being let out of the gate. All the joints of his fingers bent like that of claws. Then he picked out the longest sharpest knife from the table. He leaned over the lady whose heart was still beating, and he carved her face off.

"There, that's better, how do you like that mother? How do you like your lovely face now? Why couldn't you have done the same thing to me? Why couldn't you have had me ripped out of your womb? Why did you ever give birth to me? I hate you for having me. No child should ever be born a bastard."

Then John took his knife, and he cut her down from her neck to her pubic bone. He cut straight through her sternum. The blood squirted across him and onto the wall. Then he put down the knife and with both hands he spread her rib cage apart, to expose her beating heart.

John said, "You gave birth to a son but then ripped out his heart, now I'm going to rip out yours."

He reached down inside her and ripped out her heart and then lay the heart on the table beside him. It was still beating.

"You're still alive. Why won't you die?"

Then he cut out her liver and placed that on the table, the heart was still beating. He cut out the kidneys and set them on the table. Still, the heart was beating. Then he cut out all of her intestines and laid them on the bed beside her. The heart wouldn't stop beating.

"Die!" he said. "Die!"

He cut out her womb and put it on the table. Then he hacked at her arms and her legs. He carved her right leg all the way down to the bone. Then he folded the left and right sides of her flesh back over the cavity that he had made. He cut off both breasts and then skinned her abdomen. Then he looked at the heart on the table, it had finally stopped beating.

"There now, this time I've killed you for good."

John then placed the womb and kidneys and one breast under her head. He bent up both legs to form a triangle. Then he put the other breast by her right foot and the liver between the feet. He took the flesh he had carved off her abdomen and thighs and placed them on the table. Then he went over and picked up the dead foetus still attached to the placenta and put it in the doctor's bag then he put the heart in the doctor's bag and finally placed the Prince of Whales Plumes pin in the doctor's bag. He put all the instruments back into the bag. Then John gathered all of Mary's clothes except for the ones she had neatly folded on the table which were covered in blood. John wiped all the blood off from his naked body and threw all the clothes into the burning fireplace. Then he went over to the corner and put back on his clothes. He calmly, quietly left the room then from outside reached inside the hole in the window and latched the door.

When he left he saw Mary still standing at the entrance to the court, it was now 8:30 am, November 8th. She was standing in front of her vomit. John walked calmly past her and said, "Go to the Brittania"

And then he continued walking and went into Crossingham's. He quickly changed into a dark suit and left the doctor's bag in the room. While he headed back out, it was now 9:00 am. When he looked up the street, he saw Mr Hutchingson talking there with Mary. He knew she would be safe. He knew 'Mr Hutchinson' was really Mr Foster, Elizabeth Foster's husband. The same Frederick William Foster that was police surveyor, who was the son of Alfred L

Foster, who was the Chief Superintendent of Scotland Yard. John figured Foster would make quick arrangements to have Mary shipped off to Ireland. So, he turned back around and went up to his room. He placed the doctor's bag in a parcel; then he gathered his things and left for the castle. He handed over the parcel to one of the guards. He identified himself as one of the Hussars of Prince Albert Victor and said the gift was from the Prince to his father for his birthday tomorrow. He regretted he was out of town and couldn't attend the party. The Prince wanted his dad to receive it, but save it and open it at the celebration tomorrow.

John told the guard, "Oh, he forgot to write on it, would you mind writing on it for him? I don't have a pen. Would you write: 'To my loving Father Prince Albert Edward VII, given with much love, from your son Albert Victor Duke of Clarence?'"

John then thanked the guard and caught a train back to York to his wife, daughter and mother-in-law.

Chapter 17

Silencing Jack

John stayed stationed there in York. His wife gave birth to a healthy daughter on December 6th, 1889. They named her Lilian Mary Malthouse. And then when Albert Victor died of syphilis in 1892, John was transferred to Hove, Sussex to be in the Queen's Royal Regiment. His wife gave birth to two more sons that died soon after birth. But then on October 25th, 1895, his wife gave birth to a son that lived. They named him Percy Neville St John Malthouse. Percy was taken away by his grandmother to go live in Kent. She handed him over to Anne's brother, William Stickle Hopkins and his wife, Elizabeth. On January 30th, 1898, Anne gave birth to a healthy baby girl they named Bessie Maude Malthouse.

On November 8th, 1900, John was hospitalised for an overnight check-up to track the progression of his syphilis. He was waiting there in his hospital bed when the nurse came in and said she was going to give him an IV injection of some medicine to make him feel drowsy before the doctor could examine him.

John told the nurse, "Could you wait for a couple of minutes? I would like to have a chat with my best friend first.

His name is Frederick William Foster, and I'm sure you'll find him waiting out in the hallway."

Then the nurse went out in the hall and asked Mr Foster to come into the room. Mr Foster came into the room with the nurse. John asked the nurse to leave them in private for a few minutes. As soon as the nurse left Mr Foster said, "How did you know I was out there?"

John replied, "I knew because I've known that you've been following me for the past twelve years. Tell me, Foster, do they pay you extra to sleep with my wife?"

"How did you know I've been with your wife?" Foster asked quickly.

"Because I know everything," John replied calmly. "It's okay; I'm sure it was just part of your job. Do you love her?"

"No," replied Foster.

"I didn't either," said John, "but she's a good mother. Are you going to marry her and make sure the children never find out about me?"

"What are you talking about?" questioned Foster.

"You don't know? Oh, but I think you do. You see Victoria is very old and sick. She's going to die soon. And her son, Prince Albert Edward, is going to be made King. She's known all along that I was the son of her husband.

"She's known that I was the smartest and the best of all of his children. And like the owner of a pet that an owner loves so much but doesn't trust its care to anyone else, they order it put to sleep before they die. You see that the nurse in the hall is about to put me to sleep so that the doctor can come in and give me a lethal injection. Victoria fears what my half-brother would force me to do on his behalf. I was born with the blood of a king but trained to be the world's best killer. I am far too dangerous of an animal, a weapon, for Victoria to leave to her son. I don't blame her. I would do the same thing. Do any of my children suspect anything Foster?"

"No," replied Foster, "Bessie is just a baby, and your son, Percy, has never seen you. Lilian is also too young to think anything. But Pus, your oldest daughter, she hates you for never being around and never showing her any attention. And she hates you for leaving her mother alone all the time. I suspect that's why she likes me."

"That's good, so when my wife dies there will be no one left to know about me and what I've done?"

"No, there will be no one," Foster replied.

"Let's review it Foster and make sure we've covered all of our tracks. Barnett got married and killed his wife; he hanged for that. Dr Gull put Eddie out of his misery once his mind was so far gone that he might talk about it. After Lord Arthur Salisbury was caught in the Cleveland Street boys' brothel scandal, he wouldn't dare let on to any involvement in this, or he would be hung too. Dr Gull, well after his stroke he re-enacted the opening of the doctor's bag at Bertie's birthday party, after doing that his son-in-law, who was a doctor, put him out of his misery too. Okay, Malthouse cottage on Buck's Row. I noticed it was turned into a parking lot for the boys' school before the 1891 census came out. What about all the records, Foster, tell me about the records?"

Foster thought back and said, "In the 1861 census you were James Law, and in 1871, census you were John Carroll."

John asked, "What about my birth certificate?"

"Father unknown," Foster replied.

John asked, "The corporal?"

"Died," replied Foster.

“Abberline?” John questioned.

“I told him I’d taken care of the problem. He trusted me on my word. He doesn’t know any more than that.”

“Good, that’s good. Tell me, Foster, do you love me? You’ve given up your whole life to protect me? You would have been the head of the new Scotland Yard. You would have been the world’s most famous detective. They’re not paying you to follow me. You’ve done this all on your own, haven’t you? Tell me, Foster, what sort of job does my family think you do?”

Foster laughed and said, “They think the same of me as they do of you. They have no idea what we do with our time all day. They have no idea what I do, and no one thinks to ask. When you die, I suppose we’ll live off your pension.”

“So, you are going to marry her then?” asked John.

“Yes,” said Foster. “I would do anything for you. I promise to protect your family. I’ll make sure no harm ever comes to them.”

Then the nurse came back into the room and said: “Okay, it’s time for your medicine.”

“Just a few more minutes,” John said to her, and she replied, “Okay, just fifteen more minutes.”

Foster began to cry, “Fifteen more minutes, that is all the time left in the world to spend with the only person I’ve ever loved so much for the pureness of their soul.”

“Stop your sniffling Foster, go bring me my bag over there.”

And Foster brought him his bag. Then John took out a photograph and said, “Here, this is a photograph of me; this is the way I want you to remember me. Don’t remember me as the body lying in the coffin. Don't go to my funeral. Remember me like this."

And John handed him his photograph.

Foster said, "I don't have time to ask you all the things I wanted to learn. Like how did you know I was going to pick up on your clues? And how did you know how to leave the messages. Did you do it by chance or was it all planned or what John?"

John replied, "This is difficult to explain in just eight more minutes. So, I'll tell you a little story that you can figure out later. When I was a teenage boy, I loved the horses in the stables across from our cottage on Buck's row. I learned how to whisper to them, how to communicate with them. I could then feel the screams of the other horses behind them in the slaughterhouse. The horses were so afraid to die; they were so scared of death. I learned to slaughter horses to stop their silent screams.

"When the silent screaming stopped, they trusted me. When I was in India, I went up into the mountains of the Himalayas and trained with a Chinese Buddhist monk. He would teach me karate in exchange for me teaching him how to whisper to the horses. But we both spoke two different languages. When he learned how to whisper, and the wild horse was tamed within thirty minutes, we both laughed as we realised we must have been whispering to each other. You see almost everyone that I killed did not come to me with fear, they volunteered, they knew what was going to happen but they were miserable with their life and they wanted it to end. I reassured them it would be quick and painless and that was their biggest fear – a painful death was their biggest fear. That's every animal's biggest fear — a painful death. After

Afghanistan, when I tortured so many men there, I vowed to myself that no living creature should ever die in pain."

John then told Foster to wiggle his fingers and Foster wiggled his fingers.

Then John asked, "Now wiggle your ears," but nothing happened. "How was it Foster that you were able to wiggle your fingers but not your ears? Those are your ears, right? Your fingers wiggled because you believed they would, your ears did not wiggle because you did not believe they would. There is a life force inside me and you and the trees and the animals that are all of the same body. If I believe I can talk with a horse, I can because it is the same as believing you can wiggle your ears."

Then the nurse came back into the room and said, "Your fifteen minutes is up, I'm sorry Mr Foster you'll have to leave now."

John firmly replied, "He's not leaving; he's going to stay right here and hold my hand."

Foster quickly took out two brightly polished farthings and handed them to John, John pushed them back and said, "It's not up there, it's in here," and he held his hand in the centre of his chest, "It lies within you. My immortality has already been passed on through my blood through my son and my son's son and his son. Do not weep for me."

And then Foster held his hand, and the nurse administered medication and John fell slowly asleep holding Foster's hand. After twenty minutes of Foster holding John's hand, a doctor came into the room and asked Foster to step out for a moment. Foster stepped out, and the doctor closed the door. Then the doctor let Foster come back in. John was dead; it was quick and painless as he hoped. Foster took John's picture and wrote on the back of it:

Sergt Farrier J Malthouse Exactly on official documents

PWO 10th Royal Hussars

Cross Swords & Crown denotes the best Swordsman in Regt

Cross Guns. Best shot in Troop

Afghan Medal

Died Nov 8, 1900

Was Champion Quarter Mile

runner of all India for three years

Sergt Farrier J. Malthouse
P.W.O. 10th Royal Hussars

Cross Swords & Crown denotes best Swordsman in Regt

Cross Guns. best shot in Troop

Afghan Medal.

Died Nov. 8. 19[illegible]

Was Champion quarter mile runner of all India for three years

Printed in May 2023
by Rotomail Italia S.p.A., Vignate (MI) - Italy